S0-CBL-418

# 365

## TEN-Minute Solutions to

# SPRUCE UP YOUR HOME

# 365 TEN-Minute Solutions to SPRUCE UP YOUR HOME

## Maintain and Upgrade the Exterior of Your House

BORDERS.

Copyright © 2008

Fair Winds Press, Inc., a member of
Quayside Publishing Group
100 Cummings Center
Suite 406-L
Beverly, MA 01915
(978) 282-9590
www.fairwindspress.com


10 09 08 07 06    1 2 3 4 5

Editor: Barbara C. Bourassa
Cover design by Doublemranch.com
Book design by Sheila Hart Design, Inc.


Printed and bound in Canada

# Table of Contents

# Chapter One:
# **SPRING**

## Kill weeds naturally.

Here's an easy, chemical-free way to keep weeds from invading your rock garden. Early each spring, scatter rock salt (the same kind used to melt snow and ice) on the stone bed. The salt will soak into the ground and kill the weeds. You'll need about four 10-pound (4.5 kg) bags to treat a 25' (7.6 m) diameter circle.

## Dress up your front steps.

For a splash of quick color, set a matching pair of stately containers filled with bright flowers on either side of a front entrance to dress it up in a flash. Aim for a multi-layered effect—a tall plant in the center, lower blooms surrounding it, and trailing vines spilling over the sides. You don't have to spring for terracotta, heavy concrete, or wrought-iron urns; today's plastic and fiberglass containers come in many sophisticated faux formats that really can fool the eye. Hint: Make sure the plantings coordinate with the colors of your house.

## Plant climbing flowers along a fence.

Even pretty white picket fences imply "no trespassing." To make your yard appear warm and inviting, plant climbing flowers or vines along a fence.

## Protect plastic furniture with car wax.

A coating of car wax ensures that the furniture requires no more than a quick damp wipe with plain water to stay clean. Car wax also keeps most plastic furniture from fading in the sun.

## Plant a flowering hedge.

Robert Frost wrote "Good fences make good neighbors,"
but a flowering hedge could be an even better way to define
your boundaries. Handsome, flowering shrubs accentuate
your neighbor's yard as well as your own. Depending on your
site, consider planting forsythia, azalea, wisteria, rosemary,
lavender, viburnum, hydrangea, or privet to separate your
property from your neighbor's.

## Disguise an old concrete slab.

Concrete stain transforms drab, gray concrete into a field of color. Concrete acid stain creates a rich medley of hues to resemble marble, stone, or an artist's canvas. This is a great way to update old patios, sidewalks, and basketball courts.

## Consider resurfacing your concrete sidewalk.

Want to give a boring concrete sidewalk a pretty new face?
Consider resurfacing it with brick veneer. Hint: If you do
go this route, lay out the design first on the dry sidewalk,
to make sure you like it, before you position the brick
permanently in mortar.

## Place a turtle near your entrance.

Turtles symbolize protection in China. Display an image of
a turtle near the entrance of your home to safeguard the
members of your household and your property.

## Clear the walk.

Make sure the walkway to your home is inviting. Level any uneven pavers and consider upgrading to something more attractive (slate, brick, concrete "stones," etc.) if your current walkway is an eyesore. Make sure the path is wide enough to walk on comfortably and doesn't flood or get muddy when it rains. Keep grass, weeds, leaves, and other debris cleared off.

## Plant a decorative border along a sidewalk.

Spotlight your sidewalk by planting a border of low-growing
groundcover on either side. This provides a transition zone
into your yard. Hint: Choose durable plants that can withstand
some foot traffic. Myrtle and ivy are good choices.

## Follow your nose.

Choose fragrant blooms for your flower gardens—lilacs,
purple petunias, hyacinths, lavender, lily of the valley—to
perfume the air with delicious aromas. Hint: Don't plant
heavily scented flowers near a patio, deck, or other outdoor
seating area; your serene retreat will become a bee haven.

## Clean plastic furniture with washing soda.

Washing soda (sodium carbonate) is also known as soda ash, and you can find it in the laundry section at the supermarket. Add about ½ cup (110 g) to a gallon (3.8 L) of hot water to make a cleaner for plastic lawn furniture. Be sure to wear gloves—the washing soda can really dry your hands—and then swipe the soda water all over the furniture with a clean towel or rag. Let it work its magic for 10 minutes, then rinse it off with the hose or wipe it down with a damp sponge, rinsing and wringing it often. If the stains refuse to budge, repeat the process, but this time, leave the soda water to soak in for 20 minutes.

## Plant ornamental grasses.

Low-maintenance ornamental grasses offer an attractive alternative to formal flower beds and shrubs. Tall varieties can also serve as screens to provide privacy or define your property's boundaries.

## Soft Scrub scuff marks from aluminum outdoor furniture.

Other scouring powders will scratch, but a little Soft Scrub on a damp, soft cloth will pick up those odd scuff marks aluminum chairs and tables are prone to.

## Plant a decorative ground cover in your yard.

Here's another easy-care alternative to the standard grassy lawn—ground covers such as myrtle, ivy, sedum, and vinca require little care, just some periodic trimming to keep them in line. Ground covers also add texture and color to your property, breaking up a uniform blanket of kelly-green turf.

## Create a tropical paradise.

Why settle for the usual boring annuals that every garden center sells in six-packs? Instead, borrow a leaf from garden designers' notebooks and grow trendy tropicals. Cannas, elephant ears, ipomoea vines, flowering sages, coleus, dahlias, and many other tropical beauties will add an exotic touch to your garden beds and make it clear that you're up with the latest gardening trends. If you haven't seen some of the new, show-stopping varieties of old-time plants like cannas, coleus, and dahlias, check out the selections at better garden centers and plant catalogs and be prepared to do a double-take. These are not your grandmother's plants!

## Throw your yard a curve.

Gently winding curves add a graceful touch in a yard. Consider adding a low curved wall, curved flowerbeds, an S-shaped sidewalk, or rounded terraces.

## Add decorative items in the garden.

Position a handsome statue in a flower bed as a focal point. A statue of the Buddha or Kwan Yin is considered lucky, according to the Chinese principles of feng shui.

## Enjoy an enchanted evening.

If you like to sit outside on warm nights, choose flowers that bloom in the evening. Annuals like moonflowers, some water lilies, nicotiana (flowering tobacco), four o'clocks, and of course, the fabled night-blooming cereus and angel's trumpet (brugmansia), are just a few you might want to consider. Plants with white or yellow flowers give off a soft glow as the sun sets. Plants with gray or silver foliage, like dusty miller, artemisia, and lamb's ears, also show up well. If you live in the Southeast, you can add flowering jessamine and gardenias to your plant palette.

## Consider creating a dry stream.

If you live in an arid locale, one way to increase yard appeal is to carve out a dry stream and fill it with stones and gravel. Some people add to the effect by planting ferns and moneywort along the sides, so the foliage hangs over the banks. You might even want to add a little footbridge crossing the stream.

## Add a birdhouse for purple martins.

Purple martins eat mosquitoes. Invite these helpful birds to
hang around your house by putting up a house just for them.
They're common throughout the East, South, Midwest, and
Plains areas.

## Bathe the birds.

Invite birds and butterflies to take a bath. Put a standing birdbath in your yard, or place a few stones in the middle of a pond or stream to give thirsty winged visitors something to land on. A large stone with a scooped out impression can serve as a birdbath, too—simply fill the recessed area with water.

## Disguise a septic tank.

Here's an easy and attractive way to hide the opening to your septic tank, yet leave it accessible for pumping and maintenance. Purchase a large, fiberglass or plastic planter from a garden supply store and turn it upside down over the opening. Then lay a circular piece of glass, metal, or plastic on top of the planter to create a table. You can set a decorative plant or lawn ornament on top if you wish.

## Make sure doors open easily.

Does your front door stick or squeak? This suggests that some areas in your life may be stuck, too, according to the Chinese principles of feng shui. Adjust or repair a sticky door promptly—you can oil the hinges with WD-40 to silence them—and make sure clutter or obstacles inside don't prevent the door from opening easily.

## Clean and maintain your air conditioner's condenser unit.

The condenser unit—the part of the central air conditioner that sits outside—needs to be clean to work efficiently. Shut off the power at the unit's disconnect switch and at the main service panel. When you're sure the power is off, remove the access panels. Wearing heavy gloves, remove any debris from around the condenser coil, fan, and motor. Use a garden hose and a soft-bristle brush to wash the outer fins and coils. Draw a fin comb along the fins to straighten any that are bent. Turn the fan and watch whether it rotates smoothly. If not, tighten the screws holding the blades to the brackets. If a blade is bent, have a professional replace the fan assembly.

## Brighten door hardware with paste wax.

Wash grungy door hardware with mild detergent, then polish it with paste wax.

## Opt to preserve architectural details.

Many older homes feature attractive architectural details such as corner boards, fascia boards, ornate window frames, dental moldings, and other decorative trim. If you opt to replace old wooden clapboard, don't remove or cover up these architectural details. Ask your contractor to save the original features and fit the new siding around them in order to preserve your home's character.

## Clean the gutters.

Clogged gutters often dump water right down the foundation walls, which leads to water problems of all sorts. When the gutters are full, scoop out the debris with a garden trowel and flush out the downspouts with the hose. Put the hose down the opening and stuff a rag around it to direct water down the spout. Turn on the water and watch what comes out the end: When the clog bursts out, you're done.

## Repair sliding glass doors.

If your sliding glass doors don't open easily, you may simply need to tighten the screws in the metal tracks so they don't bind. To keep sliding glass doors operating smoothly, vacuum and lubricate the tracks.

## Restore a damaged doorjamb.

Is your doorjamb looking a little beat-up? Maybe the movers dinged it carrying in your furniture or the dog has tried to scratch his way in. If the wood is still sound (no dry rot or insect infestation), you may be able to avoid replacing the whole thing. Clean and sand the surface to remove dirt and splinters, then fill in the gouges with wood filler. Later, when the filler has dried, sand it smooth and prime and paint it.

## Replace a torn screen.

Not only is a torn screen door unsightly, it's ineffective. Replace it by gently prying off the door spline (the trim piece that holds the screen in place). Then remove the old screen and roll a new piece of screen into place. Tuck the edges of the screen into the grooves around the opening, replace the spline, and trim off the excess screen.

## Adjust doors so they open and close easily.

If the screws have stripped the wood so they can no longer be tightened completely, remove the screws and glue toothpicks around the insides of the holes. When the glue has dried, screw the hinges securely back in place.

## Avoid faux wood-grain doors.

Fiberglass doors that have been textured to imitate wood grain usually look fake. The grain doesn't show on a real wood door that's been painted, so the faux texture is a dead giveaway. If you like the convenience of a fiberglass door, choose one with a smooth surface in a color that suits your home.

## Paint the front door.

If you don't want to paint your whole house, paint the front door to give your home a fresh, new look—fast.

## Attach an attractive doorknob.

Dress up your front door with an attractive doorknob. One of the first things visitors to your home will see and touch, a distinctive doorknob makes a good first impression.

## Update your locks.

Replace old doorknob-and-lock sets that don't function properly. Doorknobs and locks represent security, and if yours don't operate adequately, they'll annoy you every time you enter your home and/or cause you to feel unsafe. Old, worn, or malfunctioning locks may cause prospective buyers to feel uneasy, too. Change them before you put your property on the market.

## Recycle leftover paint.

If there's more than 1″ (2.5 cm) of latex paint left in a can, it can be recycled. Check with your community's hazardous waste disposal facility—most operate recycling programs.

## Get your screens clean.

Window screens are magnets for dust and dirt. Vacuum the screens, and then remove them. If possible, take the screens outside and wash them with a hose and scrub brush. If not, wash them in a bathtub and set them aside to dry. Vacuum and wash the woodwork with water and white vinegar before putting the screens back.

## Make your windows sparkle.

Clean windows make the whole house look better, especially when they sparkle! Professional window washers use this simple method for making windows shine: Mix a tablespoon or two (14.8 to 29.5 ml) of original Dawn dishwashing liquid into a gallon (3.8 L) of warm water. Wipe the cleaning solution onto the window with a lint-free rag. Starting at the top of the window, use a squeegee to remove the cleaning solution. Dry the squeegee after each stroke. If the blade gets nicked, replace it right away before it makes streaks.

## Oil your locks.

Locks that stick or bind may just need a little oil. Carefully remove the entire knob and lock set, keeping the mechanism intact. If dust and dirt have collected over time, use a hair dryer to blow out particles. Then squirt a little 3-in-One Oil into the mechanism to lubricate the parts. Reattach the lock and doorknob, and operate it a few times until the oil spreads throughout the mechanism.

## Hang a wind chime near your door.

The lovely sound of wind chimes invites people to enter your home. According to the Chinese principles of feng shui, wind chimes also chase away bad vibes and attract good chi—the vital energy that brings health, wealth, and happiness into your life.

## Consider updating a porch railing.

Old-fashioned iron railings, like those that were popular in the fifties and sixties, give your home a dated appearance. To bring your porch up to speed, you may want to remove the old railings and replace them with something more imaginative.

## Refinish tarnished brass doorknobs and hardware.

Remove the tarnished pieces and soak them in a paint stripper that contains methylene chloride, following the manufacturer's directions. Lightly rub the hardware with #00 steel wool, then rinse it thoroughly. Clean it with brass cleaner, again following the manufacturer's instructions. Spray each piece with clear lacquer spray and let it dry before reattaching.

## Unstick stickers from wood doors and trim.

There are plenty of products that can remove stickers, but many of them can also remove wood's finish. Rather than risk that, soak the stickers with furniture polish and let them sit for a few minutes. They should come right off. If not, repeat the process with cooking oil, mineral oil, or baby oil. If you don't have those things on hand, rubbing alcohol works, too.

## Find a way to incorporate stained glass.

Stained glass windows have been prized for their beauty since medieval times. Installing one in your home can serve more than one purpose simultaneously—the rich colors and designs create a beautiful accent, letting in light while masking a less-than-ideal view. Have a stained glass window affixed in place permanently or hang one in its own frame in front of an existing window.

## Aim for symmetry when replacing windows.

Most homes look best when all the windows are of the same design. Don't mix double-hung windows with awning or casement styles, for instance. Also, align the tops of the windows to create symmetry. The result is harmonious rather than chaotic.

## Reglaze your windows.

Over time, the glazing compound around a windowpane will dry out and crack. Pick one window to work on for the next 10 minutes. Dig out the old glaze and brush-clean the window frames to remove dirt. Squeeze new glaze into your palm and roll it into a long, thin rope. Fit the glaze neatly around the window panes and smooth it with a putty knife, to keep your window airtight and secure.

## Dress up your mailbox.

It's amazing what a blooming clematis vine or brilliant morning glories can do for a homely mailbox. Similarly, a planting of tough perennials like hostas, daylilies, or yarrow can brighten the base of the mailbox post and turn an ugly utility into a cheerful focal point. If the ground around the mailbox is too compacted or gravelly to plant in, you can buy containers that will split around the mailbox—plant in those. Don't forget to water!

## Dispose of and store paint thinner.

Pour used paint thinner into a glass jar and let it stand until the solid material settles to the bottom. Pour off the clear thinner and reuse it. Dispose of the solids as hazardous waste.

## Replace ineffective gutters.

Ineffective gutters allow rainwater to run down the sides of your house, which may damage siding, compromise the foundation, or allow moisture to seep into your basement. If gutters have merely pulled away from fascia boards and/or downspouts, reattach them. If necessary, replace gutters that don't work properly.

## Decorate a doghouse to resemble your house.

Replicate your house in miniature for Fido with a little creativity and matching paint color. Designing your dog's digs to resemble your own creates a sense of symmetry. It's a great conversation starter, too.

## Use latticework to hide an eyesore.

Conceal an HVAC unit, gas tank, or trash cans with an attractive lattice-work screen.

## Consider adding a greenhouse.

If you live in a cold climate, a greenhouse lets you enjoy your favorite plants all year round. You can also get a jump on planting a vegetable garden by starting seedlings in a greenhouse. A greenhouse that's attached to the house can provide heat for your home—install fans to circulate solar heat into your interior. If you do have one built, make sure that at least some of the glass panels are equipped with screens to allow adequate ventilation during warm months.

## Clean your deadbolt lock.

A deadbolt lock makes a home more secure, but if the deadbolt sticks or won't go all the way into the strike plate, it doesn't protect anything. Most of the time, all a sticky deadbolt needs is a good cleaning. Loosen the screws on the cover plate of the inside latch and remove the inside and outside cylinders. Next, loosen the screws on the cover plate that surrounds the deadbolt, and remove the cover plate and deadbolt. Spray all-purpose lubricant on all the parts, then wipe away any excess lubricant. Reassemble and check the lock.

## Reinforce door locks.

Many times, burglars don't bother trying to pick or jimmy locks—they simply kick in the door. Reinforcers make this more difficult, and smart burglars will move on to easier targets. Before you go to the hardware store or home center, measure the thickness of the door so you can buy a reinforcer that fits your door. Remove the lock and slide the reinforcer over the edge of the door. Reinstall the lock, and your home is more secure.

## Install a peephole.

A peephole lets you see who's at the door before you open it, and installing one takes only a few minutes. You can find these devices at hardware stores and home centers, usually in the same aisle as the doorknobs and security locks. You need to follow the manufacturer's instructions for the model you buy, but the general idea is that you drill a hole completely through the door, then install one piece of the peephole from the outside and one from the inside. One piece simply screws into the other.

## Maintain a whirlpool tub.

Cleaning a whirlpool tub and flushing the system regularly kills the mold and bacteria trying to take up residence in the plumbing. Use a nonabrasive cleaner and plain water to remove soap residue, oils, and mineral deposits from the tub's surface. To flush the system, fill the tub with hot water and add a little dishwasher detergent. Run the pump for 10 or 15 minutes, then drain the tub and refill it with cold water. Run the pump for 10 more minutes. Check the manufacturer's recommendations. Many suggest alternating between dishwasher detergent and bleach from one month to another.

## Choose teak, redwood, or cedar when building a deck.

All three of these handsome woods are good choices for decks and porches (as well as for outdoor furniture). They withstand inclement weather conditions and require little care. Teak, which is often used in boat building, is the most expensive of the three. Don't paint a deck made of teak, redwood, or cedar. The wood ages to a pleasant color over time. Hint: Treating the wood with a sealer, however, will help keep it from warping.

## Consider pressure-treated lumber when building a low-cost deck.

Pressure-treated lumber has been specially prepared to prevent damage from insects and fungus. You don't have to paint it either. The wood ages over time to a grayish-brown color similar to cedar, and it costs a lot less.

## Fill kitchen and bathroom drainpipes.

Check under your bathroom or kitchen sink. Odds are, the hole for the drainpipe is a lot larger than the pipe itself, and the area around the pipe is leaking air like crazy. If the hole is really big, you may have to stuff it with caulk backer rope before you add the expandable foam. If it's more moderately sized (as most are), simply spray the foam into the opening and let it dry. (This helps keep out critters, too.)

## Turn off exhaust fans once they've cleared the air.

Exhaust fans recycle the air in a room, which means they remove the conditioned air and replace it with fresh air, as often as eight times an hour in the case of bathroom fans. If your home has problems with moisture, using an exhaust fan while bathing or cooking is essential. The trouble is, during heating and cooling season when you're paying to condition the air, removing it is an expensive proposition. Run the fan while you cook and bathe, but turn it off as soon as the moisture is cleared, typically about 20 minutes. If you have a hard time remembering to turn off the bathroom exhaust fan, replace the regular switch with a timer switch.

## Close foundation vents during the heating season.

Foundations over crawlspaces have vents designed to provide fresh air to that space. This ventilation is absolutely necessary during warm, humid weather, but it's unnecessary and expensive to let cold air circulate beneath your living space in the winter. Close or block your foundation vents during heating season. Note: Not every house has a crawlspace, an unexcavated area beneath the foundation of a house. If you have one, you probably are quite aware of it. If you've never heard of one, it's unlikely that your house has one.

## Reopen foundation vents in the spring.

Without ventilation, moisture could build up in the crawlspace and lead to mold, mildew, and other nasty problems. If you're not absolutely sure you'll remember, make a note on your calendar, put it in your date book, or set an alarm in your PDA.

## Keep glass spot-free.

Use one of those "rain shield" solutions such as Rain-X to keep newly cleaned outside windows from spotting. Purchase it at an automotive store, and apply it the same way you would on windshield glass.

## Buy a high-quality squeegee.

Whether you order it online from a cleaning supply house or get one from an auto supply store, invest in a high-quality squeegee that won't miss any window-washing fluid and will last for a lot of windows (even the ones on your car!). It should have a very soft rubber blade without nicks or blemishes and will cost about $10. If you're into it, buy extra rubber blades at the same time so you'll have a replacement when your current blade wears out.

## Use your squeegee in a pattern.

Squeegee the insides of your windows from top to bottom, and the outsides from side to side. That way, if there's a streak, you can see which side needs another pass with the cleaning fluid.

## Sweep and vacuum your porch, then scatter throw rugs.

The porch is the source of lots of dust and loose dirt, caused by everything from foot traffic to hanging baskets. Before resorting to a wet wash, sweep or vacuum what you can, starting with the outside walls, and moving inward to the inside walls, windowsills, and any doorframes and thresholds. Then sweep (or vacuum) any loose dirt from the floor before proceeding with any wet cleaning products.

## If upholstered porch furniture smells musty, crack open some cat-box litter.

Remove the cushions and scatter about ½ cup (65 g) of unused litter on each, then scatter another cup (130 g) or so on the base of the furniture. Let it sit for a few hours, sweep up what you can, and then vacuum up the remainder. Believe it or not, your furniture will now smell fresh!

## Soak woven rope furniture or hammocks in a baby swimming pool.

A couple of times a year wash any woven rope furniture or swings in a baby-sized plastic swimming pool. Fill it up with water and add about a cup (235 ml) of bleach and a scoop of laundry detergent—about as much as you'd use to run a load of wash. Let the rope parts soak for 10 or 20 minutes, keeping the wooden supports out of the water. Scrub any tough spots with a vegetable brush, and then remove the rope and rinse it off with a hose. Take it out of the bleach pretty fast or you'll damage it.

## Use baby powder to combat sand—while you're still outside.

Whether you've taken a trip to the beach or you walk through dunes to get to your backyard, sand can coat your skin. To avoid bringing it into the house to penetrate the hall carpet and eventually make its way to the shower floor, dust yourself with baby powder while you're still outside. The sand will fall off almost magically (okay, you'll need to dust it off with your hands a bit, too) once the baby powder absorbs the moisture holding it to your skin.

## Try a sun shower.

If you live in a sandy area or have an outdoor job or a home pool, consider getting a portable "sun shower" that attaches to your garden hose and stands up on a flat surface for a pseudo-shower before you come in the house. They're available online and at home and camping stores—make sure you buy a model that has no metal parts to corrode.

## Hide cracks in concrete.

Use durable, all-weather concrete paint to cover up small cracks in a concrete wall, floor, or foundation.

## Invest in a dehumidifier.

Dampness is a fact of life in many basements, resulting in mold, mildew, and moisture damage to insulation and wooden joists. Consider installing a dehumidifier to reduce moisture in your basement.

## Level a washer from side to side.

Washers are not meant to walk. If you've ever seen one lumber across a floor during a cycle, you know that while it's entertaining, it's also bad news for the floor or the washer. The key to keeping a washer in place is to keep it level. Put a level on top of the washer and look at the center bubble. It should be centered within the window, between the black lines. If not, you'll need to adjust the washer's front legs with a wrench.

## Vent your dryer.

An unvented dryer releases almost a gallon (3.8 L) of water into the house with every load it dries. That much moisture encourages the growth of mold and mildew, a very poor proposition. If your dryer isn't vented to the outdoors, get it done right away.

## Install dimmer switches in your workout area.

If you use your exercise area for more than one type of workout, dimmer switches will allow you to adjust lighting to suit your needs—bright lights for weight training, softer illumination for yoga or tai chi.

## Install a fan in your basement.

Sometimes all you need to keep a basement dry is good air circulation. A ceiling or wall-hung fan can help prevent moisture damage, mold, and mildew.

## Upgrade the electricity in the workshop.

Power tools use a lot of electricity. Consider upgrading your shop's electrical system to accommodate your equipment. This means installing numerous outlets at convenient spots in your shop so you'll have plenty of power when and where you need it.

## Hang a mirror to open up a dark basement room.

You can create the effect of space and light by hanging a large mirror on a wall of your basement room. The mirror imitates a window and produces an illusion of openness. You might even find a mirror with grilles that actually looks like a window.

## Choose commercial grade carpet for a workout room.

Low pile, commercial grade carpet is a good choice for a workout area. It's manufactured to stand up to heavy use, and imprints left by exercise equipment won't be as obvious as they might be on plush carpet.

## Consider building a deck over your garage.

If your home sits on a small lot and your garage has a flat roof, consider tapping the unused area atop a garage for a roof top deck. This arrangement works best when a single-story garage adjoins a two-story house.

## Use rolling shelf units in the garage.

Steel shelving units with locking casters allow you to move them about easily when necessary. Sleek and sturdy, these versatile modules are perfect for organizing your workshop, office, garage, or pantry.

## Choose carriage house doors for your garage.

Instead of the usual metal garage doors, add character to your home by choosing wooden carriage house doors or barn doors instead.

## Choose power equipment that folds up.

Some table saws, lathes, drill presses, joiners, etc., are designed to fold up and roll out of the way when not in use. If workspace is limited, a five-in-one that combines five different pieces of equipment into a single unit can be a convenient choice. This practical tool enables you to make the most of your shop's floor space.

## Install locks on storage cabinets/closets.

Safety comes first, especially if you have young children in your home. Lock up cabinets and/or closets where you store your tools to prevent the risk of accidental injury.

## Stash exercise gear in a hammock.

Keep your exercise gear neat and handy with a mesh gym hammock. Hang the hammock in the corner of your workout room and use it to corral clutter.

## Hang tools on a pegboard.

The trusty pegboard is a staple in many workshops. To keep track of your tools, draw an outline of each tool on the pegboard, to show where it belongs. If something hasn't been put back in its proper place, you'll notice immediately.

## Hang carriage lamps on your garage.

Hang old-fashioned carriage lanterns (wired for electricity, of course) to complement your garage doors. Hint: Choose lamps that seem larger than you think you'll need. They'll look smaller when affixed to your garage than they do in the showroom.

## Label your electric box.

Label the circuit breakers on your electric box to indicate which ones are linked with which functions in your home. Hint: You may also wish to draw a diagram on a separate piece of paper to show which circuit breakers operate which features in your home.

## Disguise your electric box.

Hang a picture or a large calendar over the electric box
to hide it from view.

## Divide your work areas.

Separate clean and dirty areas in your workshop. Build
a sawdust-free zone that can be closed off for painting,
varnishing, etc. Place house saws, lathes, joiners, and other
power equipment in another section of the workshop.

## Use hooks to hang rakes, shovels, and ladders.

Keep your ladders and landscape maintenance tools on sturdy hooks mounted on the wall. No more tripping over them.

## Level a washer from front to back.

The back of a washer is difficult to reach, so most washers have self-adjusting feet on the back that automatically adjust to the changes you make on the front feet. Even so, you may need to reset them after leveling the front feet. Unplug the washer and recruit a helper. Grab the back of the washer and pull it up toward you until the back feet are about four inches off the floor. Make sure everything and everyone is out of the way, and then let go of the washer. When the washer drops, the back feet should readjust themselves. Check the washer with a level again, and repeat this process if necessary.

## Hang ceiling hooks for bicycles and strollers.

If you want room to park your car, hang big items such as bikes and strollers from the ceiling of your garage. It's amazing how much floor space this frees up.

## Replace washer hoses.

Water flows into the washer through hoses that connect the water supply pipes to the unit. These flexible rubber hoses are under pressure all the time, even when you're not using the washer. Inspect them every couple of months, checking for cracks or signs of wear. They should flex easily if you bend them gently. If they're brittle, replace them right away before they burst: A burst hose sprays water everywhere and makes a terrible mess.

## Use rafters to store sleds.

Rafters or an upper level in your garage, storage shed, or barn are extremely useful for storing sleds, toboggans, and other large seasonal items, such as surfboards.

## Clean the door gasket on a front-loading washer.

Grime and mildew can build up on the rubber gasket of a front-loading washing machine door. Once a month or so, scrub the gasket with a mild non-abrasive cleaner such as 409 or Chlorox Cleanup. Rinse thoroughly and dry the gasket well.

## Use a shelving unit to store tools and gardening supplies.

If you don't have a workbench to store your tools, a shelving unit works perfectly. Keep all small tools such as hammers, mallets, and saws, off the floor and away from children. Shelves are also a great place to store your gardening supplies. But if you have mice, it is wise to hang your gardening gloves.

## Check the spin cycle on your washer.

A regular load of laundry should dry in about 40 minutes. If your dryer is working but it takes a long time to dry one load, the problem may be with the washer rather than with the dryer—the spin cycle may be leaving too much water in the load. To check, fill the washer and set the dial for the final spin. Let the cycle run for about 90 seconds, then check the tub: All the water should have drained out. If there's still water in the tub, have a repair person adjust the spin cycle.

## Store fasteners in a storage bin.

Have you gotten a tetanus shot lately?  If not, you may want
to grab those nails and screws (very carefully!) and put them in
a safe place such as a storage tray. Organize all fasteners in a
plastic tray with dividers so you can separate them by type.

## Clean the dryer vent outlet.

Whether the dryer is gas or electric, you need to check the vent outlet every month or so. Pull out any lint and make sure the outlet isn't obstructed in any way.

## Set the temperature of your hot water.

In most homes, you'll find the water heater in the mechanical area, near the furnace. A water heater is a large tank, often white or gray, with two water supply lines and an exhaust flue on top. On one side, near the bottom, you'll see a large label, a thermostat, and a dial. Before doing anything else, read the label for warnings and other important information. Then check the temperature of the water by following these steps: Let the hot water from a sink run for 4 or 5 minutes, then hold a candy thermometer in the stream for about a minute. Turn off the water and check the thermometer. Adjust the temperature of your water by setting the dial to 120°F (48.8°C).

## Get to know your electric service panel.

What you may call the fuse box or breaker box is referred
to by professionals as a service panel. Most service panels
installed in the US before 1965 use fuses to protect the
circuits; those installed after 1965 use circuit breakers. Find
your service panel and spend some time studying it. If your
system uses fuses, replace any that show signs of rust. If you
see rust inside the panel itself, have an electrician check it
right away. If your system has breakers, test them. One at
a time, turn each breaker off and back on. If you don't feel
a distinct click when you press the switch back to the on
position or if the lever feels loose, have an electrician check it
right away.

## Store auto supplies in a shelving unit.

Put those bottles of antifreeze, window-washing fluid, oil and the like on shelves, where they'll stay tidy and accessible, but out of your child's reach.

# Chapter Two:
# SUMMER

## See your yard as others see it.

That woodpile in the back may be convenient, but others may view it as an eyesore. Ditto the rusting swing set, kids' toys strewn about the yard, moldering lawn chairs, exposed trash cans, sagging fence, and collection of plastic bird feeders with squirrel guards. Especially if you're selling your house, go outside right now and spend 10 minutes really looking at your yard with fresh eyes—the way a stranger would see it. Note eyesores on a sheet of paper. Maybe that garden gnome with the chipped face isn't as cute as you once thought he was. The trellis looked great when you put it up ten years ago, but now it's falling apart. What would you do differently? Note that as well—then prioritize your improvements. This may be the best 10 minutes you've ever spent.

## Plant container gardens.

Here's a quick, low-maintenance alternative to planting a garden: Put decorative flowering plants, cacti, topiary, etc., in attractive containers and arrange them on your porch, deck, or steps.

## Attract butterflies.

Butterfly weed and butterfly bush are logical choices if you want to attract butterflies. Butterflies are also drawn to plants that offer broad, flat landing pads, such as Mexican sage, lantana, black-eyed Susan, coneflower, daisies, asters, cosmos, coreopsis, calendulas, crimson clover, and verbena.

## Reflect summer heat with white window shades.

White-colored window shades are best for regions with warm summers because they help reflect heat away from your home.

## Create a rock garden.

If you're a reluctant gardener or live in an inhospitable climate where it's difficult to grow flowers, design a rock garden instead. Put down a bed of small stones a few inches deep—round, brownish-gray river stones look more natural than standard driveway gravel. Then position larger, interestingly shaped rocks at various points as decorative accents. When you have more time to spare, you can also incorporate statuary, a bird bath, solar-powered lamps, or a few easy-care plants in containers into your design. Designate it a quiet spot for rest and reflection and include a bench or a couple of chairs where you can sit and enjoy your masterpiece.

## Don't let weeds take over the driveway.

In just a few years, weeds can cause cracks and destroy a paved driveway. Don't let them get a foothold. If you aren't against using chemicals, you can extend the life of your driveway by spraying the invaders with a little weed killer as soon as you notice them poking through the pavement. Otherwise, pull them out by the root by hand.

## Reduce soil erosion.

Keep your property from washing away. Hire someone (or set aside a day on your calendar) to build terraces in your yard to slow down water runoff and reduce soil erosion. Planting native grasses, ground covers, and hardy shrubs will help to hold the soil together, too.

## Choose plants for hanging baskets carefully.

Even if you hate to sweep up fallen petals and flowers, you can still have beautiful blooms in hanging baskets on your porch, as long as you choose the plants with care. Create baskets using mostly foliage plants like gray helichrysum, burgundy or chartreuse ornamental sweet potato vine, or caladiums. Then add colorful cascading annuals that shed very little, such as calibrachoa. Impatiens and verbena look great in hanging baskets, but they are heavy shedders.

## Just add water.

Whether it's a serene water garden with flowering water lilies, lotus, and huge, colorful koi, or a simple birdbath, a water feature can really enhance your property. Bubblers and solar fountains make small water gardens, recirculating fountains, and streams easy to operate. Or invest in the latest landscape trend—a recirculating water feature that seems to disappear into a bed of rocks like a mystical spring.

## Garden in a barrel.

Barrel gardens let you place a decorative water feature close to your deck or porch. Fill a large oak barrel with water, then add goldfish and smaller water plants, such as papyrus and water hyacinths.

## Don't take on too much.

Start small and remember the virtues of low-maintenance landscapes. Begin with the areas of your yard that show the most (usually the ones facing the street). If you have no trouble keeping these small areas looking good, gradually expand each year. Hint: Always ask yourself if you're enjoying what you're doing.

## Plant a different rose bush in your garden for each family member.

Roses traditionally mean love. When you tend to the needs of your rose bushes, you'll be reminded to tend to the needs of your family. Even if you and your family members are separated by disagreement, the rose bush (symbolized by its beautiful flowers and thorns that sometimes draw blood) is a wonderful way to connect with your roots and foster a loving heart. No need to allow the thorns to detract from the beauty of the blossoms.

## Plant red flowers in front of your home.

Because red is a lucky color in China, you can improve your good fortune by planting red flowers in front of your home. Window boxes or planters are good choices for apartment dwellers. In China, wood containers signify growth, and ceramic or stone pots represent security.

## Make paths and lay stepping-stones to reach gardens and bird feeders.

In the spring, it's essential to be able to get to and from the newly tilled earth without walking through mud. Later in the growing season, you should be able to comfortably walk out to weed and harvest without traipsing through wet grass or wet earth. As for bird feeders, consider whether you'll be refilling them in the snow or mud, and make sure you'll have a place to step neatly. (Use rock salt on the stepping-stones or footpath when you do the driveway, too.)

## Use plants to deflect bad vibes from the street.

If you live near a street, you may be getting zapped by bad vibes (known as *shar chi* in feng shui terms)—especially if your home is situated at a T-shaped intersection and cars drive directly at you. To alleviate the disruptive effects of this pattern, plant shrubs between your home and the street— they provide a visual screen and block the oncoming energies from the street.

## Add a window box.

Decorative window boxes planted with flowers add a colorful touch to any home. Paint window boxes to match your window trim or front door, then fill them with easy-care annuals that will bloom all season. Coleus, impatiens, and begonias grow well in semi-shade; nasturtiums, petunias, pansies, and geraniums add a cheerful appearance in a sunny spot. Hint: Window boxes need watering frequently—up to twice a day in very hot, dry weather.

## Attract hummingbirds.

Plant red, tube-shaped flowers—columbine, monarda (bee balm), larkspur, penstemon, lupine, nasturtium, and nicotiana (flowering tobacco)—to attract hummingbirds to your garden.

## Add an arbor.

Warm up your yard with the addition of an arbor. Plant hardy, climbing vines that will wind around the arbor and provide beauty as well as shade. Fragrant wisteria is a particularly good choice. Or you could plant grapevines and enjoy the fruit of your labors, literally.

## Consider laying stone over an old concrete slab.

If your concrete patio, basketball court, or driveway needs a facelift, consider purchasing handsome flagstone slabs in varying sizes to overlay on the old foundation.

## Use a trellis to break up blank walls.

If you have an expanse of blank, boring, or downright ugly wall with no windows, put up a trellis. You can find many styles, from lattice to wire, in garden centers, garden catalogs, and online. Later, when you have time, add flowers. Make sure you choose a trellis style and flower colors that suit your home's design and color.

## For window cleaning, head for the automotive department.

Getting ready to clean windows? Head to the automotive department and buy several gallon-size containers of windshield-washer fluid. Purchasing it this way is cheaper, as you can fill several spray bottles, and it doesn't streak easily.

## Consider the other homes in your neighborhood before painting your house.

When deciding what color to paint your home, take into consideration the other buildings nearby. Choose hues that complement and coordinate with your neighbors' homes, rather than clashing.

## Wash your front door.

Working from the top down, vacuum the frame and the door. Wash the area with mild detergent and water. Use a sponge paintbrush to clean the corners of raised panels.

## Keep ants off glass tabletops with vinegar.

If you serve lots of lemonade or sugary coffee from solid-surface tabletops on the porch, make sure to wipe them down often with undiluted white vinegar. The smell will dissipate after an hour or so, but it will keep ants off the scent of sugar for days.

## Clean up the threshold.

When cleaning the front door, don't forget the threshold. One note: Never use any product containing ammonia on an aluminum threshold. You can wash almost any threshold with mild detergent (such as Tide) and water.

## Block out the sun.

Blinds and shades block the sun and keep it from heating up your rooms. Opaque roller shades block 80 percent of the heat gain that occurs through uncovered windows, and white Venetian blinds block 45 to 50 percent.

## Use a window fan at night.

Summer evenings are often cool enough that you can turn off your air conditioner and rely on a window fan. Place the fan in the window to draw indoor air outside, and, if possible, open a window at the opposite end of the room to create a pleasant cross breeze.

## Use a chimney cap.

A cap will prevent water damage and keep squirrels, chimney swifts, and the like from nesting in the chimney. A chimney cap also keeps debris from blocking the chimney and inviting carbon monoxide into the house.

## If you can, clean your windows on an overcast day.

Windows won't streak as easily when the sun isn't shining, simply because you have plenty of time to wipe the fluid off before heat dries and streaks it on the spot. If you can't avoid washing windows on a sunny day, try to stay on the side of the house that's opposite the sun.

## Fill cracks in wood doors.

Cracks are unattractive and expensive—they leak air! Luckily, they're easy to fix. On painted doors, fill the cracks with wood filler or caulk. On stained doors, use tinted wood putty. Work on the inside part of the door first. Sand each area as you finish and then touch up the paint or stain.

## Mist your entrance with an inviting scent.

To stimulate positive feelings in those who enter your home, mist your entryway with a scent that evokes a sense of security, comfort, and welcome. Vanilla is a popular choice, because many people associate this warm, pleasing aroma with baking and nourishment. Pine and balsam scents spark images of festive winter holidays and good cheer. In the summer or in warmer regions, citrus scents seem clean and refreshing.

## Choose a house paint color that's appropriate for its style.

Each period and architectural style is associated with specific color palettes. When choosing paint colors for your home, consider using colors that are characteristic of its period, style, and locale. For example, Victorian houses, such as San Francisco's "Painted Ladies," originally sported vibrant color combinations. Only a few hues—charcoal, dark red, yellow ochre, gray, and white—are authentic to seventeenth- and early eighteenth-century Capes and saltboxes. Salmon and turquoise are perfect for Miami's Art Deco bungalows.

## Clean electrostatic filters every month.

If your system includes an electronic air filter, you need to wash the filter every month during cooling season. Use cool water and a soft scrub brush or run the filter through a light, gentle cycle in the dishwasher. Don't use the dry cycle. Let the filters air dry, then replace them.

## Know that color charts can be deceiving.

As a rule, paint samples appear darker on color charts and little squares than they will when used on exterior walls. Remember that sunlight will cause colors to look lighter, and over time, paint will fade. So opt for a darker shade than you initially think is right.

## Accentuate decorative architectural details.

If your house boasts distinctive architectural details—moldings, cornices, corner boards, pillars, etc.—emphasize them. Choose a contrasting color for the trim, instead of painting the entire exterior the same hue. Depending on your home's style, you may want to highlight interesting features by using several coordinating colors.

## Hire someone to insulate your attic.

Heat rises, so it's no surprise that an uninsulated attic is a prime source of heat loss. Not only will insulating your attic save you money in heating bills—especially as fuel costs continue to escalate in the future—experts say investments in energy-saving updates provide one of the biggest paybacks when you sell your home.

## Prevent cracks in wood doors.

Unless all the edges of a wood door are finished, it expands and contracts with the weather, which encourages cracks to form. To prevent this from happening, paint or seal all the edges of the door—including the top and bottom. You can find high-quality wood sealers in the parts department of a hardware store or home center, or at any paint retailer.

## Recharge and recycle your air conditioning refrigerant.

Hire an HVAC professional to recharge and recycle the refrigerant in your air conditioning system every two years.

## Add shelves under the eaves.

Don't waste that valuable space under the eaves in your attic. Add shelves or a shelving system for storing things you don't use often—holiday decorations, children's school projects, off-season clothing. Shelving also lets you organize your stuff and keeps it accessible so you can find it quickly when you need it.

## Patch damaged asphalt driveways.

When water finds its way under holes and large cracks in asphalt, it can wash out the gravel base and, eventually, ruin the driveway. Fill holes as soon as you notice them. Vacuum out the hole with a wet/dry vac, and then flush it with a garden hose. Fill the hole with asphalt patching material (available at home centers), mounding it slightly. Warm the area with a heat gun, and then tamp the material with a brick (or some other heavy object) until the patch is level with the surrounding area.

## Choose durable flooring for an entryway.

Carpet or wood may not be the best choice for an entryway, especially one that kids and pets use frequently. Instead, lay Mexican tile, slate, brick, or vinyl that will stand up to lots of activity.

## Keep wicker furniture clean with the hose.

It's hard to imagine, but the best thing for wicker furniture is to turn the hose on it every few weeks when it's in use outdoors or on a screen porch. Just set it on the grass and rinse it with plain water—remember to rinse the back and underside, too—and let it air-dry. To prevent wicker furniture from wearing out quickly if it's on an exposed porch, try to remember to cover it with a tarp or vinyl cover when it rains.

## Turn off your humidifier.

Ask anyone—humid air feels warmer than dry air. That's a good thing in the winter, but not in the summer. If you have a central humidifier system on your furnace, turn it off during the cooling season. You'll save the energy it uses and—more importantly—you'll be comfortable at higher temperatures, which means the air conditioner won't have to run as often.

## Patch a small hole in a screen.

There's no end to the things that can create small holes in screens, children being the first that comes to mind. Tiny holes don't seem to matter much until you realize these holes are magnets for mosquitoes and no-see-ums. Seal small holes in fiberglass screen with clear nail polish. On wire mesh screen, weave the edges of a mesh patch into the edges of the hole using a knitting needle or similar tool to push the wires in and out.

## Take stock of your attic ventilation.

It's a fact of physics: Heat will build up in your attic unless you provide an escape route. Check your attic and make note of the ventilation. Are there windows, fans, or a ventilation system that prevents excess heat from damaging whatever you've stored there? If not, call a contractor to discuss your best options.

## Make a point to paint one side of your house each year.

If you don't have the time or inclination to paint your entire house all at once, set a date this year to paint one side of it. Sunlight illuminates each side from a different angle anyway, so slight variations in color won't be noticed.

## Consider adding texture with brick or stone veneer.

Brick or natural stone, sliced thin, can be applied as a veneer to exterior walls to add visual interest. It's easier and less expensive to update old siding with veneer than with full-size bricks or stones.

## Consider adding dormers to your attic.

Don't let valuable space go to waste. By dormering your attic, you could turn unused space into an extra bedroom, home office, kids' playroom, or a "room with a view."

## Study other houses in your area to get ideas.

Go on a photo safari in your own community or a nearby town to gather ideas. Look at how other people have used colors, landscaped their yards, put on additions, and handled challenges similar to the ones you're addressing. Take pictures. If you see something you really like, ask homeowners for information—paint numbers, product names, what contractor they used, etc. Most people enjoy talking about their home improvements and will share information with you. Remember, imitation is the most sincere form of flattery.

## Use dark grout in a tiled entryway.

If you tile your entryway, choose a grout color such as gray or brown that will hide dirt.

## Consider a pull-down staircase.

If the only way to get into your attic is through an access panel, consider installing a pull-down staircase to facilitate easy access. Unless the existing access panel is in a closet, you may be able to place the new staircase in the same location and avoid cutting an additional hole in your ceiling.

## Clean brick siding.

Most dirt and stains on brick can be removed with a stiff-bristled brush and water. If that doesn't work, add a little laundry detergent to the water. Rinse the area thoroughly.

## Give your oven a break and fire up the grill.

Grilling is one of the reasons why living is easy in the summer time. It's simple and it makes food delicious. Best of all, your air conditioner doesn't have to strain to keep up with the heat created by the oven or stovetop.

## Choose the right size shutters.

Originally, shutters were designed to provide protection from the elements and intruders. Today they function mainly as decorative features. If you like the look of exterior shutters on your windows, remember their original purpose. Don't choose puny louvered panels to nail beside your windows—choose shutters that are appropriately sized and affix them to the window frames, so that if you were to close them they would completely cover your windows.

## Close the gap.

You'll often find a gap between the house sill (the top of the foundation) and the siding. If that space is open, fill it with something called caulking backer rope found in the weatherstripping aisle of home centers and hardware stores. This is an incredibly simple process—you just unroll the backer rope and stuff it into the gap between the siding and the foundation. If you push the backer rope far enough into the gap, it will stay all on its own, sealing out drafts and itty-bitty critters.

## Choose cheerful colors for your entryway.

Light, bright colors such as yellow, peach, or Granny Smith apple green make a foyer or hallway seem inviting. Because these are the first places guests and household members see when they enter your home, select paint that has a cheery hue. Bright colors will give dark mudrooms or back halls a sense of openness and warmth.

## Clean your lawnmower deck after each use.

The deck, or underside, of a lawnmower can become coated with grass clippings. When this happens, the blade can't turn easily, the motor has to strain, and the mower uses up more gasoline. Rinse off the deck of the mower after every usage. If necessary, use a putty knife to gently scrape away crusty bits.

## Patch stucco siding.

Despite its durability, stucco siding sometimes develops cracks that need to be filled before water finds its way into the walls. As long as the cracks are thin, you can fill them with concrete caulk. Overfill the crack, then smooth it out with the help of some denatured alcohol and a disposable paint brush.

## Use a rotary mower.

Gas-powered mowers are expensive to buy, run, and maintain. If you have a small- to medium-sized lawn, you can avoid that whole category of expenses by using a rotary mower. A rotary mower is nothing more than several blades on a spindle attached to a handle. As you push the mower, the blades spin and cut the grass. As long as you keep the blades sharp, these mowers work wonderfully. Consider this: With a rotary mower, you'd be doing something good for the planet and your wallet, and you won't have to pay extra for the workout!

## Provide shade for an air conditioning condenser.

Shading an air conditioning condenser increases its efficiency by up to 10 percent. Use shrubs, other foundation plantings, or a trellis to provide adequate shade. No matter what you use, make sure you leave plenty of air space to avoid restricting airflow to the condenser.

## Age cedar shingles for patches.

The color of new cedar shingles makes repairs stick out like a sore thumb unless you age the shingles before putting them in place. Dissolve a cup (125 g) or so of baking soda in a gallon of water and brush it onto the new shingles. Let them sit in the sun until their color matches the siding.

## Fill small holes or dents in aluminum siding.

Instead of patching small areas of damage with new siding, fill them with auto-body filler, which you can find at an auto parts store. You should also be able to find some auto-body paint to help blend the repair into the surrounding siding.

## Maintain your lawnmower.

Keeping the blades sharp and the oil and air filters clean helps a mower burn less gasoline and minimizes pollution. Remove the blades and take them to be sharpened once a month. Tune up your lawnmower every year before mowing season.

## Seal an asphalt driveway.

Sealing the driveway is a once-a-year or once-every-other-year job. Pick a warm, dry day for this project and wear old clothes and shoes you won't mind parting with—it's a messy job. Wash down the driveway with a garden hose or a power washer. Repair any holes and fill any cracks with asphalt patching material. Starting in a corner near the house, pour a puddle of asphalt sealer onto the driveway, and use a squeegee or old broom to spread it out in a thin layer. Work your way toward the street, one section at a time. Block off the driveway and let the sealer cure before using or walking on the driveway.

## Reflect heat from your roof.

If you live in a hot climate, choose reflective materials for your roof to cut down on air conditioning costs.

## Add folding awnings to your house.

Remember the colorful cloth awnings that graced grandma's house? These practical and attractive accents perk up homes that were built during the first half of the twentieth century. Art world giant Edward Hopper found them so appealing he made them the subject of a popular painting.

## Put a timer on your window air conditioner.

There's no reason to leave a window air conditioner running all day if you're not home to enjoy the cool air. There's no reason to come home to an uncomfortable room, either. Instead, plug the air conditioner into an inexpensive timer and set it to turn on half an hour before you get home.

## Put lockers in your garage.

If household members tend to enter the home through the garage or mudroom, add a locker, like those used in gyms, for each member. Lockers keep coats, hats, gloves, boots, etc., neatly organized and hidden from view. Kids can stash backpacks and school materials there, too.

## Remove mold from walls.

Mold and mildew are unhealthy for you and your house. Combine ¾ cup (177 ml) of chlorine bleach and one gallon (3.8 L) of plain water and apply with a clean rag or sponge. (Never mix chlorine with other cleaning chemicals.) Wear rubber gloves and make sure you have plenty of fresh air while you work: Open a window or run a vent fan.

## Mix paint with a drill.

Paint separates quickly, so it's important to stir paint right before using it. The problem is, if the paint's been sitting around too long, it takes a lot of stirring to get the job done right. Instead of a stick, use a paint-mixer bit and a variable-speed drill. It's quick and easy. Two notes of caution: First, put the drill on a low speed—you don't want air bubbles in the paint. Second, keep the head of the bit down in the paint as long as the drill's running so you don't throw paint all over the room.

## Run a dehumidifier during humid weather.

When it's hot and humid, run a dehumidifier. With less moisture in the air, you can set the thermostat higher and still be comfortable.

## Replace fluorescent lighting.

Many shops feature unimaginative overhead fluorescent lighting, but adjustable track lights offer more versatility and let you direct light where you need it most. Halogen lights provide greater clarity and less color distortion than fluorescents, too.

## Stop looking for your keys and sunglasses.

Hang a shelf in your garage so you have a convenient
place to put these things when you come inside. Hint:
You can place a small lamp on the shelf, too, to illuminate
a dark entrance.

## Remove smoke stains from bricks.

Dissolve trisodium phosphate (TSP) in water. Use the solution
and a scrub brush to clean the brick. Rinse thoroughly.

## Add pleasing colors to a workout room.

If your exercise area is dull and uninviting, you might not
want to spend much time there. By adding colorful artwork
or a bright coat of paint, you may be able to increase your
motivation to work out. Red and orange are two great
choices, as they are mentally and physically stimulating.

## Don't make the garage a focal point.

In many instances, the garage occupies a prominent position in a house's design; it may even be the first thing you notice from the curb. However, the entrance to the car's home shouldn't detract from the entrance to your own living space. If you're adding a garage or redesigning the exterior of your home, avoid positioning the garage doors so they face the street. Place the entrance to your garage at the side or back of the house instead.

## Install shelves, shelves, and more shelves.

You can't have too many shelves in a workshop, where organization is a priority. Adjustable shelves are better than stationary ones. If your garage is doing double-duty as a shop, install plenty of shelves so tools and gadgets stay neat, safe, and handy.

## Dispose of and store paint safely.

Be kind to the planet when you dispose of paint. If there's less than 1" (2.5 cm) of latex paint left in a can, leave the lid off and let it dry out. Most communities allow small amounts of dried latex paint to be thrown in the regular trash. Alkyd paint always has to be treated as hazardous waste. If there's more than 1" (2.5 cm) of paint, cover the can with plastic wrap, then replace the lid. Tap the edges of the lid with a rubber mallet to make sure the lid is on securely. Write the date and the name of the room where the paint was used on the lid, then place the can, upside down, in storage. (The paint against the lid keeps air from infiltrating the can. Just make sure the lid's on tight before you turn it upside down.) Don't let the paint freeze, and don't store it near a gas furnace or water heater.

## Hang up a workbench.

A garage or utility area can become a workshop instantly—hang a fold-down workbench on one wall. Like a Murphy bed, it closes up, out of place, when not in use.

## Schedule a tune-up for your furnace.

Just like a car, a furnace works most efficiently when its working parts are in tip-top condition. Have new furnaces checked and tuned up every two to three years; older systems should be tuned up at least every other year. Many utility companies offer this service at reasonable prices. Be sure you're getting an actual cleaning and tune-up, not just a safety check. The process should take between two to three hours and cost between $100 to $150, depending on where you live.

## Store all toys in a large plastic tote with a cover.

Store all outside toys such as balls, bats, and Frisbees in an extra-large plastic tote. It's a great way to keep your yard from looking like a playground.

## Put an umbrella stand by the door.

Keep those dripping umbrellas out by placing an umbrella stand in the garage by the door to the house. This keeps unwanted moisture out of your house, and allows your umbrellas to dry properly.

## Place a shoe mat by the door.

Put a doormat in the garage by the connecting door, and train your family to take off their wet or muddy shoes before entering the house. No more dirty footsteps all over your clean kitchen floor.

## Take stock and clear the air.

Inhaling dust, paint fumes, etc., can be hazardous to your health. Survey your workshop to make sure it has a good ventilation system.

## Raise your washer and dryer.

Put a platform under your washer and dryer to make it easier to access front-loading appliances. If your basement is damp, raising your appliances will also help prevent problems caused by moisture. Some manufacturers make companion platforms for their washers and dryers, so you may want to contact them first.

## Hang a fold-up laundry table.

A hinged panel can become a convenient table for folding laundry. Fasten it to a wall or fit it into a closet, where it can easily drop down when needed and fold up out of the way when you're finished.

## Decorate the shed.

Make your shed look as attractive as it is functional. If the shed has windows, decorate them with window boxes filled with colorful flowers. If not, plant flowers around the base of the shed to add some cheer and warmth.

## Keep small tools handy.

Hang a magnetic strip on the wall in your workshop to keep small tools handy and neat.

## Consider adding a sink in your shop.

Make cleanup easy and keep dust, paint, oil, etc., out of the rest of the house with a utility sink in your workshop.

# Chapter Three:
# **FALL**

## Get your soil analyzed.

Before you plant flowers, shrubs, or vegetables, analyze your soil for alkaline/acidity, certain toxic materials or heavy metals, and other factors. Take a sample of your soil to the county extension service, and they'll run a complete analysis for you for a minimal fee.

## Consider adding a decorative fence.

If your home is near a street or sidewalk, putting up a fence could provide the valuable illusion of privacy and safety. In most cases, a wooden picket, split-rail, or decorative wrought iron fence that's about chest-high is best. They define your personal space without appearing forbidding. Hurricane and stockade fences can make your home seem like a walled fortress.

## Keep plants neatly trimmed.

Trim shrubs and other outdoor plants periodically so they convey positive messages. Dead leaves and limbs symbolize decay, according to the Chinese principles of feng shui. Overgrown foliage suggests your life is out of control. Healthy, well–cared for plants represent a healthy, happy living situation.

## Attract birds.

Birds like shrubs and trees that produce berries and fruit. Plant chokecherry, elderberry, crab apple, or mulberry to attract birds. Sunflowers will also tempt feathered friends to visit your home.

## Prevent accidents on slippery steps.

Use textured paint on outdoor steps to produce a safer surface. Combine exterior floor enamel paint with a non-slip additive, then give stair treads two coats of paint. Hint: Rough up the surface first so the paint will adhere better.

## Fill a jar with pennies and bury it outside your kitchen.

When you follow this Chinese feng shui tip you are planting "seed money" that will grow steadily in time.

## Give your yard a nostalgic touch.

Position a decorative bench, reminiscent of those found in city parks, under a shady tree in your yard. Or hang a porch swing from the branch of an old oak tree.

## Consider adding a labyrinth.

Centuries ago, labyrinths were built on sacred sites throughout Europe and in other parts of the world. Not to be confused with mazes, these circular designs are making a comeback today; many people enjoy walking them as a form of meditation and relaxation. You can fashion your own labyrinth from stones, defining the pathways or "circuits" with larger stones laid on top of the small ones, or create a turf labyrinth by cutting the pathways into the grass. Another option is to plant small shrubs or flowers in winding rows to designate the circuits.

## Switch to organic fertilizer.

Instead of loading up your land with toxic chemical fertilizers, go organic. Bone meal, compost, cottonseed meal, mulch, and manure are safe for kids, pets, and the environment.

## Touch up scuffs and stains on plastic furniture.

Use touch-up paint for the task. The best is Krylon Fusion, a top-selling spray paint that bonds directly to most plastics without sanding or priming and dries in 15 minutes or faster. It also comes in twenty-eight colors and features the easy-to-use Touch Fan spray nozzle.

## Opt for a curved driveway.

According to the Chinese principles of feng shui, a straight driveway conducts energy too quickly from the street to your home and can produce tension. Instead, select a driveway design that curves gently toward your home, like a meandering stream or a horseshoe that allows easy entrance and exit.

## Get rid of dandelions, naturally.

Corn gluten meal is a natural herbicide that helps keep dandelions from proliferating in your lawn. It's effective for limiting other weeds, too. Best of all, it's safe for kids, pets, and the environment.

## Try a global perspective.

Here's a "what's old is new again" trend: gazing balls (also called gazing globes), those reflecting balls that are usually set up on stands. Garden designers love them because they add light, color, and an exotic touch to any landscape. Instead of breakable glass, you can buy stainless steel or copper gazing balls and leave them out all year round. Some catalogs carry solar gazing balls in swirly patterns that absorb light and release it at night. Gazing balls come in many sizes and colors, from silver and gold to luminous rainbow hues. Set them on stands, float them in water gardens, or nestle them under foliage in your garden beds. The possibilities are endless—have fun!

## Keep steps, sidewalks, porches, and decks in good repair.

This tip is both practical and symbolic. To prevent possible accidents and injuries, make sure steps, sidewalks, porches, and decks are sound and in good condition. Damage also signifies problems in other areas of your life and conveys a bad impression of you to people who see or visit your home.

## Patch an asphalt driveway.

Fill cracks, chinks, and small holes in an asphalt driveway with asphalt pitch (a mixture of coal tar, sand, clay, and water). Trowel the mixture into the breaks in the pavement, then sprinkle sand on the pitch. Drive over the patch to press it firmly into place and let it dry overnight.

## Add inviting seating.

If your yard is large enough, you can create clusters of seats with a table or other amenities, or design several different seating areas. Take advantage of a view: Site your bench or other seating so it looks at something pleasant—your house, garden, or an inviting distant view. Container plantings will add color and charm, as long as they're the same scale and style as the seating. Make sure the seating is in keeping with the style of your home and landscape. A formal group of benches would overpower a tiny yard or seem incongruous with a casual cabin.

## Hide your foundation.

If the foundation detracts from your home's appearance, hide it with an attractive ground cover that stays green year-round. Ivy, portulacaria, and sedum are good choices for camouflaging a low foundation. To add color and textural variety, grow perennials like hardy ferns, bleeding hearts, hellebores, and hostas in shady areas. Peonies, Siberian iris, and daylilies are great in sunny ones. Add bulbs—daffodils, crocus, hyacinths, tulips, and snowdrops—for early-spring interest. If your foundation is high enough, consider covering it with hardy boxwood or holly—but be diligent about keeping these shrubs trimmed. Yucca and rosemary work well in hot, dry climates.

## Take the edge off.

Plant shrubs at the corners of your house to soften those hard lines. Twining vines on trellises will do the trick, too.

## Plant an herb garden.

In Colonial times, herb gardens were a standard feature outside many kitchens. There's no reason why today's homeowners can't also enjoy having fresh herbs at their fingertips. Lots of herbs are easy to grow and don't require much space. Some, such as rosemary and chives, blossom with pretty flowers or perfume the air with a delightful scent.

## Keep up with the upkeep.

Trim shrubs, pull weeds, and rake leaves to keep your yard looking its best at all times.

## Install good lighting at your home's entrance.

Installing adequate lighting near the entrance to your home will invite chi to bring its life-giving energy your way. From a practical standpoint, good lighting also helps you and visitors find the way to your home and can prevent accidents.

## Add color with foliage.

Here's a great landscaping trick for people who want a lot of garden color without having to worry about when things will be in bloom: Use foliage to add landscape color. By putting plants with colorful foliage, like coleus, heucheras, hostas, cannas, and some of the new foliage geraniums, in containers and garden beds, you'll be guaranteed season-long color (as long as you remember to water).

## Plant some shade.

Plant trees and shrubs on the west and south sides of your house to shade your home and keep it cool. Deciduous, or leaf-shedding, trees are best because they become bare in the winter when you want the sun to shine through and warm your home. With just one tree shading your walls and roof during the afternoon, you can reduce wall and roof temperatures by 20 to 40°F (-6.6 to 4.4°C). When the walls and roof are cooler, less hot air finds its way into the house, and the air conditioner runs less often.

## Install awnings, arbors, and pergolas.

Any device that shades your windows, especially on the south and west sides of the house, reduces solar gain. If you install awnings, choose models that can be removed or retracted easily in the winter. If you build an arbor or pergola, plant trailing and creeping vines to cover it with beautiful color and add more cooling shade.

## Plant natural insulation.

Vines and shrubs growing next to the house create air spaces that help keep the house cool in the summer and warm in the winter. Install a trellis and train some vines and trailing plants to grow up it. Note: Don't train vines to grow directly on the house. Vines can damage the siding with their tendrils and suckers.

## Use sandpaper to remove rust on wrought-iron outdoor furniture.

Go over the rust lightly with fine-grade sandpaper, and then wipe off the debris with a clean, dry cloth. If you don't like how it looks after the rust is gone, use the manufacturer-provided touch-up paint, or head for the hardware store.

## Provide shade for skylights.

Plant large trees to shade skylights. These days, you don't have to wait quite as long for trees to grow—a qualified arborist with the right equipment can plant mature trees successfully. Of course, large trees are expensive, but so is cooling a room with an unshaded skylight. Talk with a local nursery and your utility company, and find out how long it will take for the energy savings to equal the investment.

## Plant shade for driveways, sidewalks, and patios.

Anyone who has ever played on an asphalt driveway or playground knows how hot it can get, and concrete isn't much better. Around your house, the heat from the driveway and sidewalks radiates up to the walls of the house and heats it up. Shading these surfaces reduces the amount of heat they reflect toward your house. Adding trees, shrubs, plants, and flowers along the sides of your driveway and walkway improves the curb appeal of your home and reduces your energy costs.

## Plant evergreen trees on the north and northwest sides of the house.

Drive through the farmlands of Iowa, and you'll see evergreen windbreaks on the north side of nearly every homestead. In some places, if it weren't for those trees, there wouldn't be a thing to break the wind for miles and miles. Although the situation at your house isn't likely to be as drastic, a row of evergreens to the north of the house will block winter winds and prevent drafts.

## Don't let dormers ruin your roofline.

Adding a shed dormer can significantly increase the amount of usable space in a house's second story. But don't destroy the original roof line. Start the dormer about a foot (30 cm) in from the edge of the roof and slope it into the roof's peak. If your home has interesting corner posts or decorative trim, reproduce these features on the shed dormer, too, for consistency.

## Think creatively when adding a deck.

Add variety to a deck by laying out floorboards to create a pattern. Zigzag, herringbone, checkerboard, or diagonal configurations give a deck more visual appeal.

## Fill cracks in wood entrance doors.

Cracks in wood doors leak an unbelievable amount of air. Luckily, they're easy to fix. Work from inside the room. On painted doors, fill the cracks with wood filler or caulk. On stained doors, use tinted wood putty. Then sand the area and touch up the paint or stain.

## Consider building a multi-leveled deck.

Another way to increase a deck's visual appeal is to vary the levels. If you're planning on adding a deck to your home, consider one with two, three, or more distinct sections, each a few steps higher or lower than the adjoining one. Before committing to a specific design, give careful thought to how each section will be used and how traffic patterns will flow from one level to the next.

## Add insulation to floors above unheated spaces.

Floors above unheated spaces, like basements and crawlspaces, can be icy cold in the winter if they're not well insulated from below. If you have unusually cold floors in a room on the first floor, check below the floor for insulation. If you don't find any, have it added.

## Check vent pipes.

Gas forced-air furnaces produce exhaust fumes, which are carried out of the house through vent pipes. Unfortunately, the condensation produced by a furnace is very acidic and can corrode these metal pipes. Corroded vent pipes need to be replaced immediately because they leak carbon monoxide, a very dangerous gas. At the beginning and end of every heating season, inspect the vent pipes for signs of corrosion. If you see anything suspicious, call an HVAC specialist or your natural gas provider.

## Maintain carbon monoxide detectors.

Test and clean your carbon monoxide detectors every month and replace the batteries once a year. Vacuum the cover, and then press the TEST button for 5 to 10 seconds. The alarm should sound. If not, replace the batteries. If the alarm is hardwired, check the circuit breaker or fuse, too. If the alarm still doesn't work, replace it.

## Caulk exterior openings.

There are all kinds of openings in the exterior walls of our houses—openings for the water supply, electricity, phone and data lines, sillcocks, and dryer vents, for example. The edges of these openings are filled with flexible caulk. When it fails, moisture, insects, and yes, even rodents have access to the house. Inspect the openings every spring and fall. If the caulk has shrunk or cracked, clean it out with a utility knife or small screwdriver. Refill the openings with butyl caulk or expandable foam.

## Give your house a bath.

Once a year, power wash your house or wash it with a long-handled brush, warm water, and a mild detergent. If you're using a power washer, direct the spray at an angle and try not to aim the spray at joints of any sort, including mortar joints. Be sure to wash below the eaves and under porches and decks. Note: Power washers produce some serious water pressure, so test the spray before directing it at the house and don't aim the nozzle at yourself or anyone else.

## Deck out your deck.

Colorful hanging baskets can add pizzazz to an ordinary deck. Choose attractive wire-and-coir-liner baskets and fill them with hanging plants that will grow well in your light conditions. Vining nasturtiums, petunias, tuberous begonias, trailing geraniums, creeping zinnias, sweet alyssum, and lobelia are good for sunny spots; ipomoea (ornamental sweet potato), and variegated ivy are better suited to shadier sites.

## Add insulation in your walls.

Consistently outrageous energy bills may be a sign that your house isn't adequately insulated, especially if it's an older home. To see if you need more wall insulation, find a flashlight and go to the main service panel. Shut off the power, and then take the flashlight to a light switch on an outside wall. Remove the cover plate and shine the flashlight into the space between the switch box and the wall. Take a look at the insulation there and estimate its thickness. If you don't find any insulation or what you do find seems inadequate, consult a professional insulation contractor. When you're finished, replace the cover plate and restore the power.

## Shop around for an insulation contractor.

Get recommendations from friends, relatives, neighbors, insulation suppliers, and home centers. Get bids and check references from at least three contractors. Before making a final decision, pick up a Federal Trade Commission (FTC) fact sheet from a local home center or insulation supplier. Ask the contractor to show you his or her calculations for proper density, and then check those calculations against the fact sheet.

## Dress up a porch.

Add interest to your porch with a decorative knee wall, a short wall about knee height, instead of an ordinary railing. Create an attractive original design or take one from a book and make a template. Hint: Simple designs, such as those used for stencils or gingerbread trim, usually work best.

## Select French doors for extra light.

Take advantage of a great view and let the light shine into your home. Replace solid doors or ordinary windows with attractive French doors. Hint: Plain frames look best on contemporary homes, and doors with grilles are better choices for older houses.

## Insulate the area above a rim joist.

The rim joist is the large board at the top of your foundation walls, the board to which the floor joists are connected. In many unfinished basements or crawlspaces, the area between the rim joist and the floor sheathing isn't insulated. You can take care of this problem remarkably quickly. Buy several batts of fiberglass insulation at your local home center (ask for unfaced, R-19 insulation). Locate the rim joist in your basement or crawlspace. Cut the insulation into strips and push the strips into the cavities above the rim joist. Note: Be sure to wear long sleeves, heavy pants, gloves, safety glasses, a hat, and a dust mask or respirator when working with fiberglass insulation.

## Combine privacy with convenience.

Many patio and French doors are available with blinds factory-installed between the inner and outer glass panes. Convenient controls allow you to open and close the blinds easily, and because the blinds are encased in glass you'll never have to dust them.

## Choose aluminum or vinyl-clad doors for easy maintenance.

Sliding glass or French exterior doors clad with aluminum or vinyl resist fading and corrosion. They don't need to be painted either. However, your color options will be limited.

## Reach for the hose when washing outdoor windows.

Forget the ladder. Use Windex Outdoor Window & Surface Cleaner. It comes in a special package that attaches to your garden hose, and then you can spray it on windows as far as your hose sprays. It does a really good job and requires no rinsing. Of course, it leaves a few spots and you can't direct the spray perfectly from down below, but it looks much better than most people could do trying to hand-wash while standing on a ladder, and it takes much less time.

## Seal mechanical openings.

The openings for water spigots, gas lines, electric service, and phone and data lines leak air unless they're filled in some way. It's easy, inexpensive, and very cost effective to plug them with expandable foam. If an opening already has filler but it's cracked or crumbling, use a utility knife to cut it out. When you've completely gotten rid of the old filler, spray expandable foam into the opening. Whenever practical or possible, spray the expanding foam from inside rather than outside the house—it creates a tighter seal.

## Choose wood doors for elegance and authenticity.

Real wood doors add a touch of elegance to any home, and are the appropriate choice for older homes, especially those built before vinyl, fiberglass, and other modern materials were available. However, a wooden door will require more maintenance than one constructed of manmade materials.

## Caulk around vents and other fittings.

Apply silicone caulk around dryer vents, exhaust fan vents, and other fittings mounted on the siding of your house. If you find old caulk there already, remove it completely before adding new caulk.

## Paint your door red, peach, or purple for good luck.

Red, peach, and purple are considered lucky colors in China. Paint your front door one of these bright hues to attract chi and good fortune to your home.

## Add caulk wherever two dissimilar materials meet.

It's a simple theory: There are bound to be gaps wherever two dissimilar materials meet, and those gaps leak air. Fortunately, a few minutes with a caulk gun will take care of those leaks for good.

## Fix stubborn window cranks.

When you turn a window crank, it drives a system of rollers, extensions, and pivots. If these parts of the tracks are dirty, the window is hard to operate. To clean a crank assembly, open the window until the roller at the end of the extension arm gets to the slot in the track. Pull the extension arm out of the track and wipe off the roller. Clean the track with a stiff brush, and wipe off the pivoting arms and hinges. Spray a lubricant on the track and hinges, and wipe off any excess. Put the extension arm back into the track and test the window. It should glide open and closed.

## Prune shrubs surrounding the air conditioning condenser.

Shade is a good thing, but restricted airflow is not. Prune any shrubs around your air conditioning condenser a few times every year to make sure leaves and branches don't restrict airflow to the unit.

## Install a pool cover.

Putting a cover over a pool between uses reduces the evaporation of water by 90 percent and reduces the cost of heating the pool since the cover helps the pool retain heat.

## Adjust a double-hung window for easy open and close.

Modern double-hung windows (the kind where the sashes slide up and down to open and close) generally don't need much maintenance but do sometimes need to be adjusted. Start by cleaning the vinyl tracks with a toothbrush and a damp rag. While you're at it, look for the adjustment screw on the track insert on each side of the window. Turn these screws, a little at a time, until the window opens and closes smoothly.

## Cover your spa and add a heating timer.

By covering your spa, you can keep the water warmer between uses. That way, less energy is needed to get it hot and steamy. You might also want to add a timer to your spa to automatically raise the temperature right before you typically use it. This way, you can enjoy added convenience and savings.

## Check building codes before putting up a railing.

Many communities have building codes that specify how high a railing must be and how much space must be left between the balusters. Before you add a railing on your porch or deck, check to see what regulations apply in your area.

## Adjust the spring tension on double-hung windows.

To adjust a spring-lift window, unscrew the top end of the metal tube from the jamb and twist the spring to adjust the spring tension. Holding the tube tightly, turn the spring clockwise for more lift, counterclockwise for less.

## Put away the garden hoses for winter.

The water in a garden hose will freeze and split the hose if you leave it outside over a cold winter. Before the first freeze of the season, take the hose off the spigot and drain it. Put one end of the hose at the top of a ladder and let the rest trail down. After half an hour or so, coil the hose and store it in the garage or basement for the winter.

## Unstick a window by cleaning the weatherstripping.

One thing that makes double-hung windows stick is dirt or paint stuck to the weatherstripping. Spray some all-purpose cleaner on a clean rag and wash the weatherstripping, working from the bottom to the top. To remove dried paint, use a clean rag and a little paint thinner. Be careful not to ruin the paint on the sashes and trim.

## Avoid faux wood-grain siding.

If you opt to use siding made of vinyl, fiberglass, or another manmade material on your home's exterior, avoid wood-grain patterns. They scream "fake." Real wood clapboard doesn't have a distinctive grain, and when painted it's virtually smooth. Choose siding with a smooth, texture-free surface for a more authentic look.

## Research your home's history.

Check your home's "pedigree" before you begin remodeling. It may appear on a local, state, or national historic register or have been designed by a well-known architect. Perhaps your house once belonged to someone notable; George Washington might even have slept there. If the building has architectural or historical significance, you'll want to maintain as much of its original detail and character as possible—like antique furniture and collectible *objets d'art*, a period home is worth more if it's restored, not remodeled.

## Unstick a window by finishing the wood.

If the window's not painted shut and the weatherstripping is shiny clean but the window still sticks, moisture may be making the wood swell. To protect the wood, all of the surfaces have to be painted or finished properly. If you find unfinished wood, that's the problem. Wait until the weather has been dry for a few days and the wood has shrunk a little, then paint or finish the wood.

## Check with your town's historic commission before renovating.

If you live in an old city that prizes its antique architecture, you may have to get the approval of the local historic commission before you can undertake exterior renovations. Some communities, such as Salem, Massachusetts, have strict guidelines that specify what's acceptable and what's not. Other towns protect First Period homes (those built before 1725) and buildings with special significance. Find out what rules apply in your area or to your house before you begin work.

## Seal leaky downspouts.

The connection between a gutter and a downspout is prone to leaks.  If you spot a leak, clean the area thoroughly and run a bead of rubber-based gutter caulk around the seam at the edges of the downspout.

## Shop for replacement windows.

If your current windows are outdated or need replacing, start shopping for new ones. Make sure the replacement windows you choose are appropriately sized and of a compatible design for your home's style and age. Picture windows, greenhouse windows, and bay/bow window sets, for instance, aren't appropriate for most houses built before 1930. Most eighteenth- and nineteenth-century houses originally featured double-hung windows, usually two-over-two, six-over-six, or nine-over-six, depending on the period and style. You don't have to sacrifice energy efficiency for authenticity—or vice versa. Major window manufacturers offer a wide range of styles and sizes to fit virtually any home.

## Cover your window air conditioning unit.

Setting up a window air conditioner is an aggravating project, which means that most people leave theirs in place year round. While this may be more convenient, it also allows air to seep in and out around the unit. Prevent this problem by placing a cover over the back of your air conditioner. Securely tape a piece of sheet plastic over the front of the air conditioner, and you'll keep your money from flying out the window.

## Seal gaps around windows.

Gaps around windows let conditioned air out and outside air in, which costs you money. To seal the window casings, the wood trim around windows, apply a bead of silicone caulk to the joint between the casing and the wall. Using the right caulk helps it blend in—clear caulk is typically best for stained trim or dark colors of paint; white or almond blends well with most shades of white.

## Maintain a room air conditioner.

Keep your air conditioner working efficiently by cleaning it every so often. Unplug the unit and remove the access cover on the front. Pull out the filter and wash it with water and a mild detergent. Let the filter dry thoroughly before you put it back inside. Remove the back panel and vacuum the condenser fins using the brush tool on a vacuum cleaner. Use a fin comb to straighten any bent fins, then replace the back cover. Now look at the back of the unit: You should find a drain hole and a drain pan just below the condenser coils. Soak up any water in the pan with a sponge or rag; inspect and clean the drain hole. Wash the drain pan with equal parts of bleach and water. When you're finished, reinstall the unit.

## Seal windows to keep in hot or cold air.

Gaps around windows let conditioned air get out and outside air get it, which costs you money. To seal the window casings (the wood trim around a window), apply clear silicone caulk to the joint between the casing and the wall.

## Close the registers in the basement.

Basements are, by their very nature, at least partially surrounded by soil, which keeps them naturally cool. Closing the register vents to the basement makes more cool air available to the rest of the house. To close the registers, simply pull the knob or adjust the dial to close the louvers beneath the cover.

## Replace or clean the furnace filter every month.

Air flows through your heating system on its way into your central air conditioning system, so it's just as important to change the furnace filters during cooling season as it is to change them during heating season. Changing the filter is simple: As you approach the furnace, look between it and the cold air duct for the old filter or filter compartment. If you don't see the filter immediately, check the owner's manual for the exact location. (You may have to remove an access cover to get to the filter.)  Grasp the old filter and pull it out, being careful not to let it catch on the sides of the blower housing. Hold the new filter so the arrow on top is pointing in the direction of airflow—from the cold air duct toward the furnace—and slide it into place. That's all there is to it!

## Use the max extract cycle on the clothes washer.

The more water in the clothes when you put them in the dryer, the longer it takes to dry them. The max extract mode on your washing machine lengthens the spin cycle and gets your clothes extra dry. Be sure to use this mode if you have it.

## Add plants to the exercise area.

Healthy plants are a quick and easy way to add to the aesthetic appeal of a workout room.

## Maintain your clothes washer.

A regular load of laundry should dry in about 40 minutes. If your dryer is working but it takes a long time to dry one load, your washing machine may not be running efficiently—the spin cycle may be leaving too much water in the load. To check, fill the washer and set the dial for the final spin. Let the cycle run for about 90 seconds, then check the tub: All the water should have drained out. If there's still water in the tub, have a repairperson adjust the spin cycle.

## Wash clothes in cold water.

Unless the clothing is heavily stained, wash it in cold water using a detergent recommended for cold-water washing. This super-simple step can save the average family up to $70 a year. Ninety percent of the cost of washing clothes comes from heating the water, so a hot-wash, warm-rinse cycle costs fifteen times as much as a cold-wash, cold rinse cycle.

## Add some pleasing scents to your workout room.

Burn scented candles or incense before or while you're using your workout room. Stimulating aromas such as clove and cinnamon can actually enhance your energy and focus.

## Presoak your dirtiest clothes.

Fifteen minutes of presoaking and 5 minutes of agitation get clothes cleaner than 15 minutes of agitation.

## Keep detergent to a minimum.

Carefully follow the manufacturer's directions regarding the amount of detergent you should use. Excessive detergent makes extra suds and those suds cause a washer to work harder and use more energy.

## Hang a full-length mirror in your workout area.

Keep an eye on your progress by hanging a full-length mirror in your exercise room. A mirror also lets you check your position to make sure you're holding that yoga posture or doing those curls correctly.

## Replace a top-loading washer with a front-loading machine.

A new, horizontal-axis (front-loading) washer can save up to $90 a year compared to a 5-year-old, top-loading washer. Front-loading washers use about half the energy and water of an equally sized top-loading washer.

## Don't stuff your washer or dryer.

Fill up your washing machine, but don't overstuff it. When it comes to drying that oversized load, it will take much longer.

## Buy a sports equipment caddy.

As always, you need to sort through what you have and discard and give away before buying anything fancy. But after that, look into a Rubbermaid sports storage bin and see if the things you have might be contained handily in one of them. The next step, of course, is making the caddy accessible to the kids so that they slowly learn to be responsible for their own equipment. Don't put it in the garage, for example, if you tend to lock it up all the time, and ensure that there's enough space around it so kids can reach to stow their stuff.

# Chapter Four:
## WINTER

## Plant evergreen shrubs near your home's entrance.

Because evergreen shrubs don't lose their foliage in winter, they symbolize longevity, health, and prosperity. Plant holly, pine, spruce, or other evergreens near your home's entrance to attract chi and keep your entryway attractive all year long.

## Graph your garden.

Before you set out to rejuvenate your garden, sketch a plan of the garden to scale. Note on the plan whatever plants you intend to put in. Because the sun's position will change and plants will blossom or die back at different times of the year, it's a good idea to make track how the sun moves across your garden for an entire year before making large-scale changes.

## Position a lion near your entrance.

Lions symbolize protection, power, and leadership. In China, statues of lions often are placed just outside the door to a building to safeguard it. Display a sculpture or picture of a lion near your entrance to guard your home and bring good fortune your way.

## Display your street address on your mailbox.

Many communities now encourage residents to prominently display the numbers of their street address so emergency services (ambulance, police, fire department) can find your home easily. Visitors to your home, delivery people, etc., will also appreciate it if you attach attractive numerals to your mailbox.

## Outfox the deer.

Hungry deer have become an increasing problem for homeowners across the United States. Without an 8-foot (2.4 m) fence (at least) and some electric wires around the perimeter of your property, it's open season on your plants. The solution? Plant things the deer won't eat. Daffodils, ornamental grasses, and thorny plants rank high on the list of foods deer generally avoid. Make your landscape challenging for them, and they'll head for the smorgasbord next door instead. Hint: Many garden centers and county agricultural extension services can provide lists of deer-resistant plants that will grow well in your area.

## Replace outdoor lightbulbs with CFLs.

CFLs (compact fluorescent light bulbs) are now available for exterior light fixtures. These bulbs have to be placed in enclosed fixtures with cold-weather ballasts if they're used in extreme climates. If the bulb will be directly exposed to moisture, make sure it's labeled "wet location listed."

## Determine the CFL replacement bulb wattage.

CFLs produce the same amount of light at lower wattages than incandescent bulbs. To figure out the wattage necessary to replace an incandescent bulb, divide the wattage of the incandescent bulb by four. For example, a 60 watt incandescent bulb should be replaced with a 15 watt CFL.

## Light up the night.

Light the way to your home with easy-to-install solar-
powered lights. Simply stick these inexpensive, energy-saving
devices into the ground along the edge of your driveway or
sidewalk—no electric wiring or batteries needed.

## Place a bowl or jar near your front door and drop a penny in it each time you go in or out.

According to the Chinese principles of feng shui, positive energy (known as chi) enters your home through the front door. Because positive chi enhances whatever it touches, it stimulates financial growth when it encounters the coins. From a psychological perspective, each time you drop a coin in the bowl, you reaffirm your intention to become more prosperous.

## Weatherstrip a garage door.

The weatherstripping on the bottom of a garage door keeps out rain, snow, dirt, and critters. If it's torn or crumbling, it can't do its job. Rolls of replacement weatherstripping are usually displayed with other door hardware in hardware and home centers.

## Add insulation to your attic.

First, check to see whether your attic is adequately insulated. Take a steel or wooden ruler into your attic and measure the depth of the insulation between the support beams, or joists. If you find 6 inches (15 cm) or less of insulation, consult an insulation contractor to see if you should add more. Utility companies in most climates recommend an insulation grade of at least R-50 for attic insulation (the R stands for resistance to heat flow). Because insulation plays such a critical part in protecting the structure of your house and maintaining lower energy bills, it's usually best to hire a professional to perform this kind of project.

## Show your numbers.

Affix shiny, new brass numerals to your front door. This little touch quickly dresses up your entrance and makes your home seem inviting.

## Remember where you come in.

It's fine to keep a grand entrance up front, complete with scrubbed porch and polished railings, but if everyone enters through, say, the kitchen or side door, that's where you should concentrate your cleaning efforts. Be especially sure to put a doormat wherever the people you consider "family" enter the house, and shake it out and/or sweep under it at least once a week.

## Cover basement window wells.

Inexpensive, easy-to-install plastic window well covers reduce heat loss from basement windows. All you have to do is measure the widest point on the window, make a note as to whether the frame is a rectangle or a semi-circle, and then buy the appropriate cover. Most designs have an upper flange that you slip under the siding and a lower flange that you simply weigh down with medium-sized rocks. After you fasten the cover to the foundation with masonry anchors, your job is done.

## Clean your doorknobs.

Clean unlacquered brass doorknobs quickly and inexpensively with Worcestershire sauce. Simply pour the spicy sauce on a soft cloth and rub away tarnish. Southwestern hot sauce cleans copper hardware just as easily.

## Increase ventilation in your attic.

If your attic doesn't have enough ventilation, truly unpleasant problems can develop, such as ice dams in the winter and moisture problems in the summer. When heat builds up in your attic during the summer, you also have to pay more to keep your house cool. Here's an easy way to find out if you attic needs more vents: Measure the attic's existing openings and then check the floor plans to find the room's square footage. The house should have at least 1 square foot (30.5 square centimeters) of vent openings for every 300 square feet (91.4 square meters) of attic floor space. If your ventilation doesn't meet this standard or if you have questions about attic ventilation, consult a qualified building contractor.

## Mount a decorative light fixture.

A distinctive light fixture positioned above or beside the front door gives visitors a good first impression when they come to your home. Choose one that reflects your personality or conveys an image you wish to project.

## Light up your life.

Make sure the foyer or front hall of your home is well-lit, not only for safety reasons, but also to give your home an inviting appearance. From the perspective of feng shui, light attracts positive energy called chi. This beneficial chi is considered to be the source of health, wealth, and happiness.

## Install motion-detector light fixtures.

While leaving the outside light on for when you return is a good idea in terms of personal security, it's not a great way to save energy. You can have the security without the expense by replacing your outside lights with motion-detector fixtures that turn on as you approach.

## Weatherstrip casement windows.

High-quality casement windows are energy efficient, but you can improve their efficiency even more by installing self-adhesive foam or rubber compression strips on the outside edges of the window stops. Tip: Use V-channel weatherstripping on windows and doors whenever possible. It takes a little longer to install than self-stick foam, but its superior performance is worth the time and trouble.

## Dress your windows in layers.

In cold weather, most of us instinctively dress ourselves in layers because it helps us keep warm. Not surprisingly, dressing a window in layers helps a room stay warm, too, and for exactly the same reason. Air retains heat, so each layer of a window treatment traps some heated air in the room. In the summer, layered window treatments provide buffers between hot outdoor air and cool indoor air. Blinds or shades covered by sheers and topped by drapes are not only stylish, they're also energy efficient.

## Buy lined drapes.

When selecting draperies, buy lined versions whenever possible. Linings help insulate the window and protect the drapery fabric from sun damage.

## Supersize your curtains and drapes.

Buy drapes, blinds, and shades that are big enough to cover the frame as well as the window itself. That way, they cut air infiltration around the trim as well as through the glass. For optimum insulation, let drapes rest below the windowsill or—even better—hang all the way to the floor.

## Add valences and cornice boards.

Valences and cornice boards add another layer of insulation above a window. Use them wherever possible.

## Weatherstrip the sides of double-hung windows.

First, scrape excess paint from the sashes and the windowsill. Cut vinyl V-channel to fit in the channel on each side of the window frame, long enough to reach two inches past the closed position for each sash. (Be sure the V-channel won't cover the sash closing mechanisms.)

## Weatherstrip the tops and bottoms of double-hung windows.

Clean the lower edge of the bottom sash. When the sash is completely dry, attach self-adhesive compressible foam. Next, lift the bottom sash and pull down the top sash. Position metal V-channel on the bottom rail of the top sash, with the open end of the V pointed downward. Nail the V-channel in place, and then flare it out to fill the gap between the sashes.

## Clean the air intake and exhaust on your forced-air heating system.

On an outside wall of the house, you'll find an air intake and exhaust. It's critical to keep the areas around the intake and exhaust free and clear. Every month or so during the heating season, remove snow, leaves, and other debris and prune any plants or bushes that might interfere with airflow.

## Replace inefficient or damaged windows.

If your home still has single-paned windows, it's time for them to go. It may seem like you can't afford to replace them, but actually, you can't afford *not* to replace them. New triple-pane windows lose 75 percent less heat than single-panes. That means lower energy bills for years to come. Be sure to replace any damaged windows as well: If condensation collects inside a double-paned window or if the glazing no longer holds the glass securely in the sash, it's time for something new.

## Weatherstrip around storm windows.

If you have storm windows, you can radically improve their efficiency with a little weatherstripping. Before hanging the storm windows, attach foam compression strips to the storm window stops on the exterior window frame. When the storm windows are in place, fill any gaps between the window and the exterior trim with caulk backer rope, weatherstripping foam designed to fill wide cracks.

## Eliminate moisture trapped between storm and permanent windows.

Water is an efficient conductor of heat, so when moisture is trapped between the windows, energy is being wasted. To let the moisture escape, drill one or two small holes through the bottom rail of the storm window.

## Install window insulation kits.

These inexpensive kits include plastic sheeting or shrink-wrap plastic to cover the inside of your window. Many kits recommend that you warm the plastic with a hair dryer to tighten it up and remove any wrinkles. Read and follow the manufacturer's directions to install.

## Lock the windows.

Even if you're not concerned about security, keep your windows locked during heating and cooling season. Locking a casement window pulls the sash tight against the frame and helps reduce drafts. Locking a double-hung window pulls the sashes closer together and blocks airflow.

## Select the best window treatment for the job.

Choose your window treatments wisely and you'll save big on heating and cooling costs. High-quality honeycomb shades with a triple cell construction, for example, are very efficient insulators, especially on windows with only one treatment. These shades can increase the energy efficiency of a single-paned window by five times, and a double-paned window by more than two times.

## Caulk around basement window frames.

Small basement windows are easy to overlook, but it's just as important to keep them airtight as it is any other window. From the outside, use exterior caulk or expandable foam to fill the gaps between the window and the surrounding block or concrete.

## Weatherproof sliding glass doors.

Apply a self-adhesive foam compression weatherstripping to the edge of the doorjamb of a sliding glass door. Now you've taken care of the edges. Unfortunately, the broad expanse of glass that makes these doors so appealing also makes them inefficient when it comes to energy. Good window treatments, such as insulated shades or thermal film, can help.

## Add a wind chain to protect a storm door.

If a strong gust of wind catches an unprotected storm door, it can yank the hinges right out of the frame. To prevent this, install a wind chain that attaches to the door frame and the door to keep the door from opening more than 90 degrees.

## Prevent drafts with a door sweep.

If the door sweep (a bristle or felt flap at the bottom of a door) is damaged or missing, cold air swoops in and energy costs skyrocket. To replace or add a sweep, start by measuring the width of the door so you can buy one that fits. Next, tack or tape the sweep in place on the inside of the door, positioned to touch the floor but not interfering with the door's operation. Drill pilot holes and drive screws to hold the sweep in place.

## Make sure exterior doors close tightly.

A door that doesn't shut tightly can allow inside air to escape. Adjust the door latch and strike plate on exterior doors to make sure they close as tightly as possible. Open and close the door, and watch the action between the bolt on the door and the strike plate, or catch, on the frame. If they're not aligned and working smoothly, try to determine which part is causing the problem. If the strike plate needs to be higher, drive 3-inch (7.5 cm) wood screws into the top of the doorjamb to pull up the doorframe; if it needs to be lower, drive the screws into the bottom of the jamb to pull the doorframe down. If the problem appears to be with the latch bolt, remove the door and set it aside. To raise the latch bolt, install thin cardboard shims behind the bottom hinge so it raises the whole door. To lower the door and the latch bolt, install shims under the top hinge.

## Learn how to caulk like a pro.

The more skilled you are in caulking, the more energy you will save. Make sure you know how to do it right before you begin. For exterior caulking, all you need is a caulking gun with a racheted plunger. To load the gun, pull back on the plunger and drop the new tube of caulk in the barrel, back end first. Pull the trigger or push the plunger until it reaches the back of the caulk cartridge. Next, cut off the end of the nozzle. The further back you cut, the larger the caulk bead will be, so decide what's appropriate for the task at hand, and cut off the tip of the nozzle at a 45 degree angle. Break the seal on the tube by sticking a small screwdriver into the opening of the nozzle and you're ready to apply the caulk.

## Prevent condensation on the inside of windows.

During cold weather, condensation forms on the room side of windows when the indoor air is too humid. If you're using a humidifier, turn it down or off. If that doesn't solve the problem, run a dehumidifier. (It's rare to need a dehumidifier in cold weather. If you do, make sure the clothes dryer is vented to the outside and that every member of the family is using the vent fan when they shower or bathe. If the problem continues, consult a heating and cooling contractor.)

## Remove condensation between removable glass panels.

Condensation forms between the panes of glass in windows with interior removable panels when the breather holes in the sash get plugged with dust or dirt. Use a pipe cleaner or small wire to clean out the holes in the bottom of the sash and the condensation should disappear.

## Use caulk wisely.

Caulk works best on cracks that are less than ½ inch (1.2 cm) wide. Wider cracks generally are best filled with expandable foam or filled with some type of backing material before you caulk.

## Test your smoke detectors.

Smoke detectors save lives, but only if they work. Test them every month and after any extended absence. Press the test button for five to ten seconds, and then release it. If the alarm sounds, press the reset button. If not, replace the batteries. If that doesn't solve the problem, check the wire connections. If the connections are secure and the detector still isn't working, have an electrician replace it.

## Adjust the door closer on the storm door.

Automatic door closers keep storm doors from slamming closed. At least, they do if they're properly adjusted. To adjust the closer, find the adjustment screw, typically on the side that faces toward the door handle. Tighten or loosen the screw and test the door until it closes completely but gently.

## Weatherstrip an exterior door.

Weatherstripping fills the gaps at the edges of a door to prevent drafts. Worn or missing weatherstripping costs you money every day. Self-adhesive products are easy to use, but it's really worth the effort to install metal weatherstripping. Measure the height and width of the door opening and cut the metal strip to fit. Tack the strips to the doorjamb and to the header, inside the stops. To keep the channel from buckling, work from the top down. When the strips are in place, use a putty knife to pull them into position, between the door and the jambs, when the door is closed.

## Purchase a new, energy-saving water heater.

Old water heaters may not be adequately insulated, so you waste energy keeping water hot. Replacing an outdated, inefficient water heater could save you money in the long term.

## Turn off the water heater when you're away.

When you're away for four days or more, you save more by turning off the water heater than you spend heating the water from room temperature when you return. Before you leave for an extended absence, set the control on the water heater to OFF.

## Install a programmable thermostat.

A programmable thermostat automatically adjusts the temperature according to the settings you've programmed. Setting the temperature back just 10 degrees for eight hours at night and another eight hours during the day while you're at work can cut your energy bills by 20 percent.

## Get help remembering to replace the furnace filter.

Some thermostats signal when the furnace filter needs to be replaced. If you have trouble remembering to replace the filter, install a programmable thermostat with this helpful feature. Also, keep in mind that while standard furnace filters work adequately, pleated filters and electrically charged filters remove finer dust and can be cleaned and reused rather than discarded.

## Clean all cold-air returns.

Forced-air furnaces require a constant flow of air, and cold-air returns are a big part of that flow. Look around any room in the house. You should see a large register cover somewhere on a wall, 6 or 8 inches (15 or 20 cm) from the floor. That's a cold-air return. Keep your cold-air returns clean and make sure they're not blocked by furniture or draperies.

## Clean all heat registers.

If you have a forced-air heating system, every room in your house has heat registers, small vents through which the heat flows into the room. Heat registers are usually in or near the floor, and there's almost always one near every window and door. At the beginning and end of the heating season, pull off each register cover and vacuum the cover itself. Next, reach down into the heat duct and clean it as far back as possible. Replace the register covers and your job is done.

## Control the flow of heat.

Every heat register cover has a device used to open or close the vents behind the fins. Some have a dial and others have a knob, but they all have some way to control the flow of heat through the register. Open the vents to introduce more heat into the room; close them to limit the heat. Because heat rises, you may want to close the vents on upper floors and open them on lower floors to direct more heat to colder areas.

## Clean your radiators.

A clean radiator is an efficient radiator; so clean yours at least once a month. Close the valve and let the radiator cool, then use the brush tool on your vacuum cleaner to dust the surface of the radiator and a lamb's wool duster to clean between the fins. After dusting, wash the radiator with warm water and a little detergent.

## Refinish your radiators.

Too many layers of paint reduce a radiator's efficiency. If your radiators are clogged with paint, strip and refinish them. To increase the amount of heat a radiator puts out, paint it a dark color, and then place a piece of aluminum or sheet metal behind it.

## Test the humidity of your air.

It's easy to find out if you need to add humidity to the air in your house. Take a glass and three ice cubes into a bedroom or living room—any room other than a kitchen or bathroom. Wait 3 minutes. If water beads up on the outside of the glass, the humidity level is fine. If not, the air is too dry.

## Keep your sense of humidity.

Because water is such a good conductor of heat, humid air feels warmer. By keeping the air at a comfortable humidity level, you can keep the thermostat turned down low and still feel comfortably warm. Consider running a humidifier, adding some living plants to your home, or leaving the exhaust fan off while you shower once in a while.

## Caulk gaps between the floor and the baseboard.

On hard floors, such as vinyl or hardwood, the baseboards are often finished out with quarter-round trim. If there are large gaps between the baseboard and the floor or the baseboard and the quarter round, you've got air leaks. You can either caulk the gaps or, depending on how large the gaps actually are, pull off the quarter round, fill the gap with expandable foam, then replace the trim.

## Insulate outlets and switches on exterior walls.

Switch and outlet boxes are set into wall cavities, which means they can leak air, especially when they're located on exterior walls. Next time you're at a hardware store or home center, pick up some insulating gaskets and fix this problem. Simply remove the screw that holds the cover to the box, press the gasket in place around the switch or receptacle, and replace the cover. You should be able to do several rooms in 10 minutes, and the whole house in less than an hour.

## Choose and use space heaters wisely.

Space heaters make sense when you're trying to keep heating costs down, but some can be dangerous. Buy them wisely and use them carefully. Radiant heaters are the most efficient type of space heat, and the best ones power down when the room reaches the desired temperature. Always keep fabric, paper, and other combustible materials well away from space heaters, and unplug them when you're not using them.

## Insulate your hot water heater and pipes.

An inexpensive water heater blanket and some foam pipe sleeves can make a big difference in the amount of money you spend on hot water. Don't overlook this easy way to save energy.

## Freshen your clothes washer once a month.

Unless you use your washer every day, it can develop unpleasant odors. There are several things you can do to control odors and keep your washer fresh. First, if you have a top-loading unit, leave the lid open between loads. Second, run the empty washer through a cycle with hot water, detergent and bleach once a month or so.

## Choose lighting for the exercise area that emphasizes warm tones.

Fluorescent lights produce cool illumination, which is less flattering to most skin types than warm, incandescent light. To give yourself a rosy glow, use incandescent or full-spectrum light bulbs in your workout area.

## Consider insulating your basement.

A cold, dank basement can sap heat from your home. By adding insulation under the floor, you'll keep heat in and drafts out. Spray foam insulation could be a better choice than fiberglass batting—it's easier to install and less likely to become damaged by dampness.

## Clean your electronic air filter.

If your heating system includes a built-in electronic air filter, it will need to be cleaned every month to keep air flowing efficiently into the furnace. Remove the filter and use cool water and a soft brush to scrub it clean, or run it through the dishwasher on a light, gentle cycle. Do not use the dry cycle. Let the filter air dry before you replace it.

## Do a few loads of laundry in a row.

Doing several loads of laundry, one after another, is cheaper than doing a load here and there. Drying consecutive loads takes advantage of built-up heat in the dryer, which saves energy.

## Separate the garage into functions.

You'll never get a leg up on garage storage if your kids' stuff is mixed in with the exercise equipment, lawn mower, and all the other car supplies that make their home in the garage. Even if you're only chipping away at the task 10 minutes at a time, make sure to start putting the kids stuff in one area of the garage, grouping "like with like" as all the organization experts recommend. That makes it easier to evaluate the fate of the items you're trying to organize and also easier to hold older kids accountable for keeping it neat.

## Weatherstrip the bottom of a garage door.

Garage door weatherstripping, which comes in rolls, is usually displayed with other door hardware in hardware and home centers. To install it, open the garage door until the bottom is within comfortable reach. Pry off the old weatherstripping and remove the nails. Line up the new piece and nail it in place. When you reach the edge of the door, cut the weatherstripping to fit.

## Use your dryer's advanced shut-off features.

If your dryer has a humidity sensing shut-off or a temperature-sensing control, use it. Compared to the traditional timed shut-off, a humidity sensing shut-off uses 15 percent less energy and a temperature-sensing shut-off uses about 10 percent less energy.

## Mix up your lighting in the workout room.

Track lights or canisters recessed into the ceiling are usually the best choices for an exercise area, allowing you to direct light where you need it. This kind of lighting will also keep electrical cords from tripping you up. Plan your work out zones first, then position lighting so it illuminates each zone adequately.

## Seal heat ducts.

Large metal ducts carry warm and cool air throughout the house, delivering it to individual rooms. These ducts have seams, and those seams leak air if they're not sealed. In areas where the ducts are exposed, such as those with unfinished or suspended ceilings, you can seal the seams in a heat duct in under 10 minutes, using hybrid tape that combines a thin layer of putty with an aluminum foil facing or pure silicone caulk. Pay special attention to the areas near the furnace, especially the joints between the duct and the furnace itself.

## Heat the basement naturally.

Sealed heat ducts will leak less air into the basement, making your basement even colder. You may want to insulate and add a vapor barrier to the basement walls to make up for the loss of heat. If you seal heat ducts in an unheated crawlspace, you may also want to wrap plumbing pipes with electric heating tape to keep them from freezing.

## Calculate and compare.

If you have your heart set on a new appliance and have reasons for making the investment beyond the energy efficiency of a new model, by all means take the leap. However, if your main reason for considering the investment is energy efficiency, you should know exactly how much your current model costs to run. Check your most current electricity bill to find cost of a kilowatt-hour of electricity. Next, check your appliance's serial plate and look for the wattage. (If the wattage isn't listed, check for amps and volts. Multiplying the amps by the volts gives you the wattage.) Multiply the appliance's wattage by the hours it will be in operation each month. Divide this number by 1,000. The number you get is the number of kilowatt-hours the appliance uses each month. Finally, multiply the kilowatt-hours by the rate your electric company charges. The result is the cost of running the appliance for a month. Compare this to the cost of running a new model and consider how long it will take for the energy savings to equal your investment in a new model.

## Know the facts before you buy.

Side-by-side refrigerator/freezer models use about 7 to 13 percent more electricity than freezer-on-top or freezer-on-bottom models. Although through-the-door dispensers and automatic icemakers seem like a good idea from an energy standpoint, many utility companies warn that they actually increase energy usage.

## Unplug unused refrigerators.

Unplugging an old, unused refrigerator in your basement or garage takes just a second, but it can save up to $170 a year! Just remember to store your unused refrigerator safely, so children can't get trapped inside. Padlock the door closed or block the door open to keep kids safe.

## Insulate water pipes.

Hot water loses heat as it travels from the water heater to the faucet. Insulating the water pipes can reduce energy costs, especially if the pipes run through unheated spaces, like crawl spaces. Purchase sleeve-type foam insulation at your local hardware store or home center. Close off the hot water supply and wait for the pipes to cool before insulating them. The foam sleeves are slit lengthwise, so all you have to do is open the tube and fit it around the pipe. Be sure to cover at least the first 10 feet (3 m) of the hot- and cold-water pipes leaving the water heater, and all pipes running through uninsulated spaces.

## Turn up the water heater before filling a tub.

To cut down on the cost of bathing in a tub, turn up the thermostat on the water heater to 140°F (60°C) about an hour before you start filling it. Start with a tub full of room temperature water and then add just enough 140°F (60°C) water to make it comfortable. As soon as you finish your bath, turn the water heater's thermostat back to 120°F (48.8°C).

## Re-position your refrigerator.

Refrigerators should be positioned away from heat sources, such as ovens, heat registers, and windows that receive direct sunlight. Allow at least two inches (5 cm) of clearance around the unit so air can circulate around the condenser coils and disperse the heat they generate. Keep your refrigerator in a temperature-controlled area. Refrigerators use much more electricity and work less reliably in an unheated garage or utility space.

## Seal the joints between heat ducts and heat registers.

Heat ducts run through cavities in the floors, ending at the heat registers. Warm air can leak between the edges of the duct and the floor if those edges aren't sealed. Again, this is easy to fix. Pull off the register cover and use hybrid duct-sealing tape to seal the edges of the duct to the edges of the floor.

## Don't use duct tape for ducts.

If you grew up believing you can do anything with duct tape, this might shock you: Duct tape is great for everything except sealing ducts. Duct tape will come apart within a few years, and you'll have to go through the whole process again. Other tapes create a more permanent seal, which saves both time and money. Look for special tape that carries the Underwriter's Laboratories logo, a symbol that indicates the tape meets or exceeds recognized performance standards.

## Move items that block air circulation.

Warm air works most efficiently when it can circulate freely. Keep furniture and draperies away from heat registers and radiators.

## Let your clothes air dry.

Here's another great energy-saving laundry idea: remove clothing when it's partially dry and let it air dry. You'll use less energy drying the clothes and you'll also avoid having to iron them!

## Use the door, not the overhead garage door.

If you come in and out through the garage door, even when
it's not necessary, it uses up electricity and allows hot or cold
air to infiltrate the garage, where the air then tries to find
ways inside the house. During heating and cooling seasons,
avoid using the overhead garage door as an entrance or exit.

## Remove lint from your dryer filter.

Lint restricts the flow of air through the filter, and restricted airflow reduces efficiency. That explains why it costs 30 percent more to run a dryer with a dirty filter. Save yourself some money by cleaning the filter after every load.

## Clean your electric dryer vents.

Dryer lint is extremely flammable, so keeping dryer vents clean is critical. At least once a year—once a season if you do lots of laundry—clean the dryer's vent system. Unplug the dryer or turn off the power to the circuit. Pull the dryer away from the wall and disconnect the vent hose from the wall vent as well as the dryer itself. Use the brush attachment on a vacuum cleaner to remove dust and lint from inside the dryer. (You may have to take off the back panel. Check the owner's manual for instructions.) Use the vacuum cleaner or a lamb's wool duster to clean out the vent hose. Replace the hose, put the dryer back in place, and restore power.

## Hang snow tires on hose mounts.

Mount a few garden-hose holders on your garage wall—they're the perfect size to hold a tire. You can hang up your snow tires in warm weather, and your regular tires come winter.

## Flush the water heater.

Water heaters that gurgle and burp are calling for help! They're being choked by sediment, which makes them less efficient and can eventually clog the drain. To remove sediment, turn off the unit. If the heater is gas, set the gas valve to 'pilot'; If it's electric, turn off the power to the circuit. Connect a hose to the spigot at the bottom of the tank. Put the other end of the hose in a sink or on a floor drain. Close the valve on the cold-water inlet, and pull up the lever on the pressure-relief valve. Turn on the spigot, but be careful—the water coming out will be hot! When the water runs clear, turn off the drain valve and remove the hose. Put the lever on the pressure-relief valve down and open the valve on the cold-water inlet. Elsewhere in the house, turn on a hot-water faucet (on the top floor, if you have more than one) and let the water run until it flows steadily, with no air bubbles. Turn the water heater back on.

## Prevent sediment buildup in the water heater.

To keep sediment from building up in the water heater, drain a gallon (3.8 L) of water from it each month. This project only takes a few minutes, but it can prevent big problems from happening later on.

## Insulate your water heater.

Put your hand on the outside of your water heater. If it feels
warm, installing an insulating blanket on the sides and top
of the heater will help it retain more heat. If it feels cool, it's
well insulated on the inside and doesn't need a blanket. Note:
Always check the manufacturer's recommendations before
insulating a gas water heater.

# Index